THE LATE
HENRY MOSS

BY **SAM SHEPARD**

★

★

DRAMATISTS
PLAY SERVICE
INC.

THE LATE HENRY MOSS
Copyright © 2002, Sam Shepard

All Rights Reserved

SPECIAL NOTE

First produced by Magic Theatre, San Francisco, CA, 2000,
Larry Eilenberg, Artistic Director.

New York premiere produced by
Signature Theatre Company, New York City,
James Houghton, Founding Artistic Director;
Bruce E. Whitacre, Managing Director.

THE LATE HENRY MOSS was first produced by the Magic Theatre (Larry Eilenberg, Artistic Director) in San Francisco, California, on November 7, 2000. It was directed by Sam Shepard; the set design was by Andy Stacklin; the lighting design was by Anne Militello; the costume design was by Christine Dougherty; the choreography was by Peter Pucci; and the production stage manager was Michael Suenkel. The cast was as follows:

HENRY MOSS .... James Gammon
CONCHALLA .... Sheila Tousey
EARL MOSS .... Nick Nolte
RAY MOSS .... Sean Penn
ESTEBAN .... Cheech Marin
TAXI .... Woody Harrelson
FUNERAL ATTENDANTS .... Rod Gnapp, Dennis Ludlow
MUSICIAN .... T Bone Burnett/Jerry Hannan

THE LATE HENRY MOSS received its New York premiere by the Signature Theatre Company (James Houghton, Founding Artistic Director; Bruce Whitacre, Managing Director) in New York City on September 24, 2001. It was directed by Joseph Chaikin; the set design was by Christine Jones; the lighting design was by Michael Chybowski; the original music and sound design were by David Van Tieghem and Jill B.C. Du Boff; the costume design was by Teresa Snider-Stein; and the stage managers were Catherine Bloch and Don Bill. The cast was as follows:

HENRY MOSS .... Guy Boyd
CONCHALLA.. Sheila Tousey
EARL MOSS .... Arliss Howard
RAY MOSS .... Ethan Hawke
ESTEBAN .... Jose Perez
TAXI .... Clark Middleton
FUNERAL ATTENDANTS .... Michael Aronov, Tim Michael
MUSICIAN .... Luke Notary

3

CHARACTERS

HENRY MOSS
CONCHALLA
EARL MOSS
RAY MOSS
ESTEBAN
TAXI
FUNERAL ATTENDANTS
MUSICIAN

PLACE

The outskirts of Bernalillo, New Mexico.

TIME

Late 1980s.

THE LATE HENRY MOSS

PRELUDE TO ACT ONE
(DRUNKEN RHUMBA)

Lights go to black on set. In the dark, very sultry Mexican rhumba music comes up. A white spotlight hits the couple of Henry Moss and Conchalla wrapped in a tight embrace, cheek to cheek. They are amazingly drunk and yet synchronized in tight, fluid coordination with only the occasional stumble and foot crunch to give them away. They begin extreme down left on the apron in front of the set and careen their way across the stage, doing a couple of twirls and deep waist bends along the way. Their cheeks stay pressed together the whole time, and they seem oblivious to the world. The dance is brief and somewhat shocking. They disappear off right. Spotlight goes to black, then lights ease up on set to begin Act One.

ACT ONE

Scene: Night. A run-down adobe dwelling on the outskirts of Bernalillo, New Mexico. The roof is open; just bare, rough-plastered walls. A mesquite door with black iron hinges in stage right wall. A deep-silled window up right. A single cot-like bed set horizontally into a small alcove, center of upstage wall with a small barred window directly above it, like a jail cell. There is a blue curtain on a rod in front of the bed that can be opened or closed by hand and sometimes mechanically. The curtain is open for now, revealing the corpse of Henry

Moss, a man in his late sixties. He lies face up on the bed with the crown of his head toward stage right. A heavy Mexican blanket in yellow and red designs covers him from the forehead down to his ankles. Over the blanket a white sheet has been spread smoothly. Only the top of Henry's head and his bare feet are revealed. Nothing is seen of his face. There is an old-style bathtub with claw feet upstage left of the bed. A sink, gas stove and small refrigerator are set against upstage wall; all very run-down and dirty. Extreme downstage left of center is a simple round Formica table with two metal S-shaped chairs set across from each other; one upstage right, the other downstage left. Earl Moss, Henry's oldest son, sits in the downstage chair with his back partially to audience, thumbing through an old photo album of Henry's, studying the pictures. Ray Moss, Earl's younger brother, stands upstage of the table, facing audience and idly going through an old red tool chest of Henry's placed on the table in front of him. A bottle of bourbon sits in the center of table with two plastic cups. An ashtray; cigarettes. Nothing else. Long pause after lights come up as Earl thumbs through album. Ray fiddles with tools.

EARL. *(Thumbing through album.)* Well, you know me, Ray — I was never one to live in the past. That was never my deal. You know — You remember how I was.
RAY. Yeah. Yeah, right. I remember.
EARL. But, these days now — I don't know. Something like this — Outta the blue. Maybe it's age or something.
RAY. Age?
EARL. Yeah.
RAY. Whose age?
EARL. Mine.
RAY. Oh. I thought you meant his.
EARL. No — me. Gettin' older. You know. I mean at eighteen, nineteen, my mind was going in a whole different direction. You remember how I was. *(He suddenly sings:)*
    Gonna tie my pecker to a tree, to a tree.

6

Gonna tie my pecker to a tree.

You remember that? *(Pause. Ray just stares at him.)* Well, do ya?

RAY. I thought that was him. I remember him singing that.

EARL. That was me!

RAY. Oh.

EARL. 1956, '57? When was that?

RAY. What?

EARL. When I used to come home singing that.

RAY. I don't know. Musta been later.

EARL. Not that much later. Couldn't a been. Ripple wine and Mexican Benzedrine! Those were high times, Ray! High old times. *(Pause.)*

RAY. I remember you leaving. That's all I remember.

EARL. *(Looking up at Ray.)* What? When?

RAY. When you first left. When the big blowout happened.

EARL. Big blowout?

RAY. You know what I'm talkin' about. *(Pause. Earl stares at him.)*

EARL. Ooh — that. Way back.

RAY. Yeah.

EARL. Way, way back.

RAY. That's still very vivid with me. Like it happened yesterday.

EARL. *(Going back to album.)* You shouldn't let that stuff haunt you, Ray.

RAY. I remember the windows exploding.

EARL. Exploding?

RAY. Blown out. Glass everywhere.

EARL. Ooh — yeah. That was *him (Gestures to Henry.)*, not me. That was him doing that.

RAY. Yeah. Him.

EARL. You're getting me mixed up with him.

RAY. No I'm not. I know it was him.

EARL. Well, don't get me mixed up with him.

RAY. I'm not. I know it was him.

EARL. Good. *(Pause. He thumbs through album.)* *He* was the one breaking windows. Not me.

RAY. I know that. *(Pause.)* What brought it on exactly? That was never very clear to me.

EARL. Oh, come on, Ray —

RAY. What?

EARL. You mean after all this time — after all these years — you still don't know?

RAY. No. I never knew.

EARL. She locked him out of the house. You knew that, didn't you?

RAY. Um — I don't know. Yeah, I guess.

EARL. Set him right off. Went into one of his famous Wild Turkey storms. You knew all about that.

RAY. I remember it like a war or something. An invasion.

EARL. Yeah, well things get embellished over the years. You were a kid.

RAY. So were you.

EARL. Yeah, but there was a certain — maturity about me. I was coming into my own back then.

RAY. Explosions. Screaming. Smoke. The telephone.

EARL. Explosions? There weren't any explosions, Ray.

RAY. People running. You were one of them.

EARL. What?

RAY. Running.

EARL. I never ran!

RAY. Mom was running.

EARL. He had her trapped in the kitchen! Under the sink! How could she run? Huh? How could she possibly run? You've really got this screwed up, Ray. You oughta get this straightened out, you know. It's time you got it straight. It's no good carrying the wrong pictures around with you the rest of your life. They're liable to get more and more warped as time goes on. Pretty soon you'll start to forget how it really was.

RAY. You ran. I watched you.

EARL. I never ever ran!

RAY. You climbed into that '51 Chevy and took off. That was the last I saw of you for seven years. Things like that you don't forget. They mark time. For *me* they do.

EARL. *(Returns to album.)* Yeah, well — I never ran, I'm not a runner. Never have been. *(Pause.)*

RAY. Seven years. Thought I'd never see you again. I thought about you all the time but I bet I never once crossed your mind. Never once.

8

EARL. That's not true.

RAY. Maybe once.

EARL. Once or twice.

RAY. Once, maybe.

EARL. I sent you something every Christmas. Most every Christmas, I did.

RAY. Yeah.

EARL. Socks. T-shirts. Rubbers. I sent you Camels once.

RAY. Tokens. Tokens of guilt.

EARL. *(Looking up.)* Guilt? Look — buddy boy, I had a lot on my mind back then.

RAY. Yeah.

EARL. I was heading somewhere. *(Long pause. Earl goes back to album. Ray fiddles with tools.)*

RAY. What should we do with his tools?

EARL. You want 'em? You might as well keep 'em.

RAY. I don't work with my hands anymore.

EARL. Oh? Since when?

RAY. I don't know. It just faded.

EARL. That's a shame, Ray. You were good with your hands. You used to be under a car all day long.

RAY. What car?

EARL. Some car. I don't know what car. Some car or other.

RAY. I never had a car.

EARL. Well, whose car was it, then, you were always working under?

RAY. It was his car.

EARL. Okay.

RAY. It wasn't my car.

EARL. Fine.

RAY. Well it wasn't. I never had a car. You were the one with the car.

EARL. All right! It was *his* car, it wasn't your car! Who gives a fly-ing fuck whose car it was! I just seem to remember, Ray, that you always liked working on cars and I thought you might like to have the tools in case you wanted to pursue that. That's all. Simple as that. *(Long pause. Earl goes back to album. Ray handles tools.)*

RAY. Looks like they're all pretty cheap anyway. Taiwan steel. Swap meet stuff.

9

EARL. You oughta to keep 'em, Ray. For his sake you oughta keep 'em.

RAY. For his sake?

EARL. Yeah.

RAY. He's dead.

EARL. I know he's dead.

RAY. So why should he care?

EARL. He won't care, Ray.

RAY. So it'd be for *my* sake, not his sake.

EARL. Yeah. For your sake. You never can tell when the urge might come up again.

RAY. What urge?

EARL. To work with your hands! That urge! The urge to be useful again. *(Pause.)*

RAY. *(Looking at tools.)* They're not worth diddly.

EARL. That's not really the point, is it, Ray. I mean nothing he's got is worth diddly. Not like we're inheriting a legacy here.

RAY. Ratchet's pretty nice. *(Ray picks up a very large ratchet wrench and fits a socket onto it.)*

EARL. Why don't you keep that, then? He'd like that, Ray.

RAY. Keep the ratchet?

EARL. Yeah. Keep the ratchet. It's a nice one, right?

RAY. A single big-ass ratchet? What am I gonna do with a single ratchet?

EARL. Work on your Buick! I don't know.

RAY. I don't have a Buick.

EARL. Goddammit, Ray!

RAY. Well, I don't. You want me to say I have a Buick just so you can feel good about giving me these crummy tools? They're not your tools anyway. You don't own the tools.

EARL. I know I don't own the tools!

RAY. They're his tools.

EARL. I know that.

RAY. They're not yours to give away.

EARL. They're not yours either!

RAY. They're nobody's tools! *(Ray slams the wrench back into the toolbox. Long pause. Earl goes back to album. Ray turns upstage and stares at Henry's corpse, then turns back to Earl.)* Well, don't you

10

think it's about time we notified someone? We can't just sit around here. Who're you supposed to call first? The cops?

EARL. The cops? What're you thinking about?

RAY. Who, then? The mortician? The Chamber of Commerce? Who?

EARL. *(Back on album.)* I'm not ready yet. *(Pause.)*

RAY. *You're* not ready?

EARL. No. I'm not.

RAY. Well, how long are we gonna wait?

EARL. *(Looks up.)* What's the rush? Huh? I'd like to spend a little time with him if you don't mind.

RAY. Time?

EARL. Yeah, time. Before he's rushed off and processed into the funeral business. Before they apply the makeup and formaldehyde and dress him up in his Air Force khakis.

RAY. Well, how much time do you need, Earl?

EARL. I'll let you know.

RAY. Haven't you been sitting here with him for a long time already?

EARL. I'll let you know, Ray.

RAY. What've you been doing just sitting here with him all this time?

EARL. Nothing.

RAY. Have you been talking to him, Earl?

EARL. He's dead.

RAY. Yeah, but when you're alone like this — just sitting here — just the two of you — You can start to make stuff up.

EARL. What stuff?

RAY. Stuff in your head. You can start — imagining things.

EARL. Like what?

RAY. Well, like for instance — you could imagine that he's still alive; he can still hear you — Maybe it's even better that way.

EARL. What way?

RAY. Imagining. I mean that might be even better than if he were actually alive because now you can really tell him things. You can tell him all kinds of things that you couldn't tell him before because now he's dead and you're imagining him to be alive and there's nothing he can do about it but listen.

EARL. I wasn't talking to him, all right! I wasn't imagining anything! I was just sitting here! Alone. With him. Just sitting here in the dark. Alone. *(Pause. Ray turns upstage and starts to move slowly toward Henry's body.)*
RAY. We can't just bury him ourselves, huh? Just dig a hole and do it ourselves? That's illegal, isn't it?
EARL. Yeah, every death has to be reported these days. Unless you kill somebody.
RAY. We could report it *after* we bury him.
EARL. They'd just dig him back up.
RAY. I mean, that's what you'd do with a dog —
EARL. What?
RAY. Just dig a hole and bury him.
EARL. Yeah.
RAY. So how come you can't do that with a father? *(Moves in closer to Henry's corpse. Earl pours himself a drink, smokes and keeps thumbing through album.)*
EARL. I don't know. I don't know the answer to that, Ray. I don't know why that is. Nobody cares about a dog. I guess that's it.
RAY. *(Getting very close to Henry.)* Nobody cares about a dog.
EARL. Well, they don't.
RAY. You mean outside the dog's little circle of friends? His little family.
EARL. Yeah, nobody cares. *(Ray reaches out to touch Henry's corpse. Earl stands suddenly.)* Don't touch him! *(Long pause. Ray stares at Earl.)*
RAY. What?
EARL. Just don't touch him.
RAY. Why is that, Earl?
EARL. Just — don't. It's not a good idea. *(Pause. Ray looks at corpse, then back at Earl.)*
RAY. Am I gonna catch something — some disease?
EARL. Just — get away from him.
RAY. Have *you* touched him?
EARL. No.
RAY. It's not gonna hurt anything, is it? *(Ray goes to touch the corpse again, but Earl makes a strong move toward him.)*
EARL. Don't touch him, Ray! *(Ray backs off.)*

12

RAY. What're you so jumpy about?

EARL. I'm not jumpy.

RAY. Are you superstitious or something?

EARL. I just don't think it's a good idea to touch him.

RAY. Afraid he might come back to life?

EARL. That's pretty funny. *(Pause.)*

RAY. He's starting to stink, Earl. I think he's starting to stink.

EARL. I can't smell it.

RAY. Yeah, well, you've been with him too long. You've grown insensitive to it.

EARL. Insensitive. *Me,* insensitive?

RAY. Yeah. There's a stink in here. There's definitely a stink and you can't smell it.

EARL. That's right.

RAY. How long's it take before things really start to rot? You know —

EARL. How should I know? I'm no expert on death. *(Earl returns to table, sits and goes back to album.)*

RAY. I mean really bad — turning to maggots.

EARL. We're not gonna wait *that* long, for Christ's sake! Just try to relax a little, Ray. All right? Just relax. Feel honored that we have this small time alone with him. Try to treasure it. *(Pause.)*

RAY. Honored?

EARL. That's right, *honored.* Somebody else could've discovered him first. Anybody. A total stranger. The taxi driver or that crazy chick — what's her name — or — anybody. They'd have called the cops right off the bat. The mortuary boys would've been here already with a body bag and hauled him off. And there we'd be. We'd be the last ones notified. No privacy. All kinds of questions. Forms to fill out. We'd never have had two seconds with him by ourselves. *(Pause.)*

RAY. What taxi driver?

EARL. What?

RAY. What taxicab driver?

EARL. The taxicab driver. The guy who picked him up and took him fishing. The guy who brought him back.

RAY. Same guy?

EARL. Yeah. Same guy. I told you that. I told you all about that on the phone.

RAY. Well, if he picked him up and brought him back, how would he have discovered him dead? He would've had to die in the taxi.

EARL. I was just saying that as an example!

RAY. It's not a good one.

EARL. I was just using the taxicab driver as an example of anyone! How it could've been anyone other than us who found him first!

RAY. Who did find him first?

EARL. *I* found him first! I told you that. You never listen.

RAY. And you just decided to sit here with him.

EARL. Sit here until you got here. I figured it was my duty.

RAY. Your duty?

EARL. That's right, my duty.

RAY. "Duty and honor, duty and honor." Doo-wah, doo-wah, doo-wah duty.

EARL. Go fuck yourself, Ray. *(Pause. Earl goes through album.)*

RAY. So, who's this crazy chick?

EARL. What?

RAY. This crazy chick you mentioned as one of the possible candidates who might've found him first?

EARL. His girlfriend.

RAY. His girlfriend?

EARL. Yeah. Whatever her name was — "Conchita" or something.

RAY. "Conchita"?

EARL. Something like that.

RAY. "Conchita Banana"?

EARL. Don't get cute. Have some respect for the dead. I went through all this stuff with you before on the phone. Don't you ever listen to anything?

RAY. I was in shock.

EARL. Well, snap out of it! *(Pause. Ray slowly circles table around Earl's back, then returns to the chair across from Earl and slowly sits. He pours himself a drink.)*

RAY. *(As he crosses behind Earl.)* I'm still in shock. I wasn't expecting to be in shock but I guess that's the thing about shock.

EARL. What?

RAY. It's unexpected, you don't see it coming. You just find yourself in the grips of it. You do the best you can.

EARL. *(Focused on album.)* Why don't we take a walk or something, Ray? This New Mexican air might just do us some good.

RAY. *(Seated with drink.)* I know this is probably going to irritate you a whole lot, Earl, but would you mind going back through the whole story for me one more time?

EARL. What story?

RAY. The stuff this guy — what's his name? The neighbor?

EARL. Esteban?

RAY. Yeah — Esteban. That's it. The stuff this guy, Esteban, told you on the phone when he called you in New York. *Before* you found Dad dead. What happened just before? I'm a little lost here. *(Pause. Earl pushes the album away and with a long exhale, stares at his brother.)*

EARL. What's the matter with you?

RAY. Me? Nothing. Nothing's the matter with me. I'm his son. You're his son. I've got a right to know, as much as you do. We're both blood.

EARL. I told you everything already, once!

RAY. Yeah — Yeah, you did. But there's some stuff that doesn't make sense.

EARL. What stuff!

RAY. There's all these — all these people you mentioned. It's just too — stupid! It's stupid that he died like this! Out here in the middle of nowhere with no — contact. No contact whatsoever!

EARL. That's the way he *lived!* He lived with no contact. Why shouldn't he die the same way? *(Pause. Ray drops his head slowly and stares at the table. Earl stares at him.)* All right — All right. Once more and that's it. I can't keep going through this, Ray. It's not something I enjoy.

RAY. Why would you enjoy it?

EARL. I *don't* enjoy it! That's what I'm saying.

RAY. Then why even bring it up?

EARL. Goddammit, Ray, you are such a little piss-ant.

RAY. That may be. That may well be. A "piss-ant." I'd just like to hear the story again, Earl. The whole story. *(Pause. Earl stares at him, then begins.)*

EARL. I got the phone call. Collect. Esteban says he's worried about the old man.

RAY. This was a week ago or something?

EARL. That's right. A week ago. About a week. Before I called you. Now listen up! Try to pay attention this time.

RAY. I'm all ears.

EARL. He's worried — Esteban. He's the neighbor. He says Dad got some money in the mail. Henry's cashed a check that came in and he's walking around with this cash burning a hole in his pocket.

RAY. Where'd the check come from?

EARL. Who knows. G.I. check or something. Government pension. I guess he was always getting these checks and going on binges. He's buying booze with it. He gets a haircut. He hitchhikes down to the shopping center. He wanders around downtown, drunk. Then he wanders down to the gas station and buys a fishing license.

RAY. Drunk?

EARL. Yeah, drunk. What else? Then he hitchhikes back out here and calls a taxi from Albuquerque. Taxi picks him up and he takes off for a day and goes fishing. He comes back that night with this Indian chick.

RAY. The crazy one?

EARL. The crazy one. *(Ray motions for Earl to continue.)* So, the taxi waits for him and the woman. Esteban sees the cab outside, so he comes over with some soup.

RAY. Soup?

EARL. That's right. Soup, Ray. That's exactly right. Esteban was always bringing Henry soup or chili or some damn thing. Trying to sober him up. Esteban says the woman's in the bathtub, giggling. She's half-naked and drunker than skunk. Esteban drinks with them but Dad won't eat the soup. They have a big argument about the soup and Henry kicks him out. Esteban stays outside by his trailer and keeps watching the house. He sees Henry come out with the Indian woman wrapped in a blanket. She's still giggling. They pile into the taxi and take off. That was the last he saw of him.

RAY. So when you get here, after the phone call from this neighbor — I mean, I'm trying to put this all together — How many days did it take you to get here?

EARL. You mean after the phone call?

RAY. Yeah.

EARL. I don't know — three or four.

16

RAY. Three or four days?

EARL. Yeah. I guess. I don't know.

RAY. It took you three or four days after you hear that he's in trouble?

EARL. I had some business to take care of!

RAY. Business? What kinda business, Earl?

EARL. Packaging! I got a packaging business now. We make boxes.

RAY. So after your "packaging business" you fly down here, walk in the door and find Henry dead in his bed? Is that it?

EARL. Yeah. That's it! Just like that. Just how he is right there. I haven't touched him. He was laying there stroked out on his back just like he is right now. All I did was cover him up. *(Long awkward pause. Ray gets up and goes to the window. He stares out. Earl watches him.)* So — How's the family? *(Ray doesn't move from window. Keeps his back to Earl.)*

RAY. What family?

EARL. Your family. Out west.

RAY. I don't have a family.

EARL. Oh — I thought you got married and uh — somewhere I heard you got married.

RAY. I never had a family.

EARL. Oh — *(Ray turns toward Earl but stays near window.)*

RAY. How's *your* family?

EARL. I don't have one either. You know that.

RAY. How am I supposed to know that?

EARL. Have I ever mentioned a family to you?

RAY. No — but I thought maybe —

EARL. Maybe what?

RAY. Maybe you had a secret family.

EARL. A secret family?

RAY. Yeah. *(Pause.)* No?

EARL. No.

RAY. That's too bad, Earl.

EARL. If I had a secret family, why would I tell you about it?

RAY. Because I'm your buddy, Earl. I'm your little buddy. You can tell me all your secrets. *(Pause.)*

EARL. Look, Ray — There wasn't much either one of us could do about this. You know that. He was on his way out. Been that

17

way for a long time. Pickled. Pissing blood. The shakes. Blackouts. Hallucinations. There was all kind of signs.
RAY. Signs.
EARL. Yeah. He stopped eating for one thing. *(Pause. Ray crosses over to refrigerator and opens it. It's completely empty except for a small jar of jalapeño peppers. Ray takes the jar out, closes fridge, crosses to table and sets jar on it.)*
RAY. Jalapeños.
EARL. Can't stay alive on peppers and hooch. *(Ray opens jar, sits at table and starts eating the peppers, chasing them down with bourbon.)*
RAY. How do we get ahold of this taxicab driver?
EARL. What?
RAY. The taxicab driver who took Dad fishing.
EARL. You got me. You have to find out what company it was first.
RAY. Well, Esteban would know that, wouldn't he? The friendly neighbor? He saw the cab.
EARL. Well, yeah, but — good luck finding the driver.
RAY. Shouldn't be that hard. They keep records. Every car has a number. Every driver. It's the law. They log in, they log out.
EARL. What's the taxicab driver gonna tell you?
RAY. I dunno. Something. Maybe he saw something. *(Earl slides the album toward him, showing him an old photo of their father as a boy. Ray doesn't look at it: just keeps chewing on jalapeños.)*
EARL. Look at this. Here he is with his dog, Gyp. Look at that. "1931" it says. 1931. So, he's how old there? How old would he have been?
RAY. Maybe he'd know how to find that Indian woman.
EARL. *(Still with album photo.)* Well, let's see — that's thirty — no — fifty-seven years ago? So — fifty-seven — he would've been — he would've been twelve years old there. Twelve years old! Imagine that!
RAY. Maybe she saw something.
EARL. So who's president then? Hoover? Or was it FDR?
RAY. Maybe she can tell us what happened.
EARL. Look at that. There he is. No idea what's in store for him. Just a kid standing in a wheat field with his dog. *(Ray slams the jar of jalapeños on the table and stands.)*
RAY. Why did he suddenly take it into his head to go fishing, Earl!

Why is that? You don't take a taxicab to go fishing! Why is he suddenly up in the mountains with an Indian chick fishing! It doesn't make any sense! I woulda gone fishing with him! Why didn't he call *me* to go fishing! I love to fish! Why didn't he call *me*! *(Pause. Earl just stares at him.)*

EARL. You were far away, Ray. *(Pause. Silence. The door swings open wide and Esteban, a small, skinny Mexican man in his fifties, very neatly dressed in khaki pants, light pink shirt with dark blue tie and shiny black shoes, is standing in the doorway holding a large green bowl of steaming soup with both hands. He smiles broadly at the brothers and just stays there in open doorway. Earl stands quickly from table and moves toward him.)* Esteban! Come on in.

ESTEBAN. Is Mr. Henry here? I saw the light on.

EARL. Come in, Esteban. Good to see you. *(Esteban begins to cross, very slowly, toward table, keeping his eyes glued to bowl of soup, careful not to spill a drop. It takes him a very long time to reach his destination.)*

ESTEBAN. *(As he crosses slowly.)* I brought Mr. Henry his soup. He sometimes will eat. Sometimes not. Depends on his mood. How you catch him. I was very worried this time. He just disappear like that.

EARL. *(Closing door.)* Esteban, this is my brother, Ray. He just — came in from California.

ESTEBAN. *(Keeps moving, eyes fixed on bowl.)* Glad to meet you Mr. Ray. *Mucho gusto. (Ray nods, stays where he is by window. Earl crosses to table, ahead of Esteban, and moves the album to make room for the soup's arrival. Esteban keeps smiling and inching slowly across the room with soup. Crossing slowly:)* I put vegetables and chorizo in there for his blood. Habañeros. I know how the blood can get from liquor. I was a drinking man, myself. Many years. Oh, yes. They couldn't stop me. Nobody. Many people weep for me but I could not hear them. Bells rang in all the chapels but I was deaf.

EARL. Do you want me to take that for you, Esteban?

ESTEBAN. No, no, no — I can manage, Mr. Earl. Many bowls I have balanced across the road for Henry. Many years of practice. The timing I know by now. The soup it cools down just right from my trailer to his door. Henry no like it too hot. One time he burn himself so bad he almost kill me. It was funny but he almost did.

I could see the murder in his eye. Real murder. The pain had made him crazy. I tell him, is such little pain, Mr. Henry. Don't kill me for such a little pain as this. Wait for a bigger pain to kill me! *(He laughs, then stops himself when he sees he might spill the soup.)* But he was drunk — so he no laugh. He no laugh with me.

RAY. Who is this?

EARL. Ésteban. *(Pronounced incorrectly with accent on first syllable.)* The neighbor.

ESTEBAN. *(Pronounced correctly.)* Estéban.

EARL. *(Repeats the mispronunciation.)* Ésteban. *(Esteban finally reaches the table and sets the soup down very carefully. He smiles and sighs with relief, then pulls a soup spoon and napkin out of his back pocket and sets them neatly beside the bowl. He pulls a salt shaker out of his back pocket and places it in front of the soup. Pause. Earl looks at Ray, then back to Esteban, who is smiling broadly.)*

ESTEBAN. So — is Mr. Henry home now from fishing? I was very glad to see the light here. Very, very happy. I was afraid he might just — vanish.

EARL. He's — He's sleeping, Esteban. Worn out, I guess.

ESTEBAN. *(Looks toward Henry's corpse.)* Ooh. *(Lowers his voice to a whisper.)* That is good. He need that. He need that after fishing. *(Esteban tiptoes over to Henry's bed and looks at corpse.)*

EARL. Don't uh — Don't disturb him now, Esteban.

ESTEBAN. *(Keeping distance from Henry.)* Oh, no.

RAY. Yeah. Don't touch him, whatever you do. My brother's liable to go ape-shit. *(Ray crosses to table, sits; pours a drink.)*

ESTEBAN. *(Whispering, looking at Henry.)* No, he need sleep. He need plenty of that. More than soup, he need sleep.

EARL. Yeah, he could use some sleep.

ESTEBAN. I bet you — *(He giggles.)* I bet you that big crazy woman wore him out. You know, Mr. Earl? That Indian woman. *(Laughs.)* She is so — you know — *(Cups his hands under his chest.)* — Robusto! No? Very strong woman. Right, Mr. Earl? A lot of woman for Henry.

EARL. Yeah — I don't know.

ESTEBAN. He have fun with her I bet. *(Giggles and sways.)* She bend his back like a willow tree. She fuck him silly. *(Esteban bursts out laughing and jumping up and down.)*

EARL. Don't do that — Don't wake him up. Okay, Esteban? *(Esteban quiets down and goes back to whispering. Ray watches from the table, somewhat perplexed.)*
ESTEBAN. Oh, no. No, no, no. He need his sleep. That is good for Henry. I was so worried when I saw he have that money. So much money. That is why I call you, Mr. Earl.
EARL. I'm glad you did, Esteban.
ESTEBAN. So much money in his hand. It is no good when a man is fighting his weakness. Too much money. *(Esteban sneaks up closer to bed and stares at corpse.)* He sleep very peaceful. Very still.
EARL. Yeah — He's exhausted.
ESTEBAN. I can barely hear him breathe. Maybe the blanket's covering his nose too much. *(Esteban moves as though to lift the blanket away from Henry's face. Earl leaps at him.)*
EARL. Don't touch him! *(Esteban leaps back away from Henry and stands there in shock. Pause.)*
RAY. *(To Esteban.)* I tried to warn you about that.
EARL. I'm sorry, Esteban — I'm just uh — I'm a little worn-out myself. *(Esteban stays frozen where he is, staring at Earl. Earl moves toward Esteban but Esteban backs up from him.)* Why don't you uh — have a seat or something. It's okay, Esteban. Everything's fine. *(Pause. Esteban keeps staring at Earl.)*
RAY. Esteban — you live right across the road here, is that right? You're the neighbor?
ESTEBAN. *(Turning toward Ray.)* Yes, sir.
RAY. How long have you lived over there, Esteban?
ESTEBAN. Thirty years.
RAY. Thirty years.
ESTEBAN. *Más o menos.*
RAY. Thirty years in a trailer.
ESTEBAN. Yes, sir, Mr. Ray.
RAY. So, you've known my father for a good long time then.
ESTEBAN. Yes. Sir. Ever since he move here from California. When he have that bad time.
RAY. Which bad time was that, Esteban?
ESTEBAN. When he think the world was trying to eat him.
RAY. What?
ESTEBAN. When he think — He was doomed, he said.

21

RAY. He said that?
ESTEBAN. Yes, sir. I have times like that myself but Henry never believe me. He think he was the only one.
RAY. Doomed?
ESTEBAN. Yes, sir.
RAY. Can it with the "sir" shit, all right! I'm not your "sir."
EARL. Take it easy, Ray.
RAY. Well, what does he think this is, the military or something? I don't need that "sir" stuff.
EARL. He's just being polite, you idiot! It's a rare thing these days.
RAY. Polite?
EARL. Politeness. It's okay, Esteban. *(Pause.)*
RAY. You want a drink, Esteban? Me and my brother have been kinda gettin' into Henry's bottle here a little bit.
ESTEBAN. Oh, no, no, Mr. Ray. Thank you, no. I no touch liquor no more. No more for me. *(Giggles.)* Is finished. Too many beautiful women have leave me. Now — when I need them most, they are gone. And I am sober. Is funny, no?
RAY. Yeah. That is pretty funny. *(Pause.)* So, you don't drink at all? Is that the story, Esteban?
ESTEBAN. No, sir. No more for me.
RAY. Well, my brother was just telling me you knocked one back now and then with the old man.
ESTEBAN. *(To Earl.)* Oh, no, Mr. Earl! I pretend with Henry. Only pretend. He never notice. *Muy borracho! (Turns back to Ray.)* Long as I make the motion, you know. *(He mimes taking a drink.)* Tilt the glass; bend the elbow — That is all he cares. Just the motion. He like the company, your father. He like the human — smell.
RAY. So, you mean — that night, when the taxi came to pick him up, you were just *pretending* to drink with him? You were — *(Mimes drink.)* just pretending?
ESTEBAN. Taxi? Oh, yes. Pretending. *Sí.* Only pretend. *(Pause. Ray looks at Earl, then back to Esteban.)*
RAY. And uh — Henry just kinda went along with that, I guess, huh? He was so happy to be in your company — So starved for human companionship.
ESTEBAN. *(Laughs.)* He was very drunk, Mr. Ray. Very, very

drunk. Like a mad dog.

RAY. And this — woman — "Conchita" or whatever her name was — she was very drunk too? Very, very drunk?

ESTEBAN. Conchita? *(Pause. Esteban turns to Earl. Earl shrugs.)*

EARL. I don't know. He just doesn't get the picture, Esteban. I been trying to explain it to him —

ESTEBAN. "Conchita"? *(Laughs.)* "Conchita," no! You mean Conchalla. Conchalla Lupina! No, "Conchita."

RAY. Conchalla Lupina?

ESTEBAN. *(Laughing.)* Sí! Eso.

RAY. *(To Earl.)* Conchalla Lupina? Sounds like an opera singer.

EARL. Does kinda, doesn't it. Conchalla Lupina.

ESTEBAN. Conchalla! She is — *magnífica!* You would not believe this woman, Mr. Ray.

RAY. Is that a fact.

ESTEBAN. She is — She is — How do you say it? Your father will tell you. She has — a big reputation down here in Bernalillo. *(Laughs.)*

RAY. Is that right? How'd she come by that? *(Esteban stops himself. He and Earl exchange looks. Pause. Ray stares at them.)* What's going on between you two? Something's going on here.

EARL. Nothing's going on.

RAY. Something's going on. What's the deal with this woman?

ESTEBAN. Oh, Mr. Ray — Conchalla is very mysterious woman. With a woman like this, believe me, a man could die in her arms and thank the saints! He could pray for no better way to leave this suffering world.

RAY. Yeah, I'd like to meet her.

ESTEBAN. They say she has done men in like that. The lucky ones. Can you imagine something like that?

RAY. Something like what, Esteban?

ESTEBAN. Oh, you know, Mr. Ray. You know — *(Esteban begins to gyrate his pelvis and go into frantic laughter, holding his stomach, then he suddenly stops. Ray stares at him.)* Oh, I am sorry, Mr. Ray — I get — when I think of her I — If you saw her you would know. She would burn a hole right through your heart! Right here! *(Stabs his chest with his fingers.)* Right through the center of your soul! Right there! *(Esteban pokes his finger hard into Ray's chest, then*

23

quickly backs away. Short pause, then Ray leaps out of chair and grabs Esteban by the collar.) Oh — I am sorry, sir.

RAY. *(Shaking Esteban.)* What'd I tell you about that "sir" shit! Huh? What'd I fuckin' tell you! *(Ray shoves Esteban backwards. Esteban trips back and falls to the floor.)*

EARL. *(Going to Esteban.)* Hey! What is the matter with you, Ray? You gone nuts or something?

RAY. I warned him! I told him about that "sir" stuff. I don't like the implication.

EARL. *(Helping Esteban to his feet, brushing him off.)* What implication? What're you talking about?

RAY. I haven't done anything to earn that kind of respect from him. That's something you say to someone you respect. He doesn't know me from Adam. How does he know I'm somebody he should respect?

EARL. Well, he knows now, doesn't he?

RAY. Yeah. Yeah! Maybe he'll think twice before going around calling strangers "sir." Who does he think he is, calling me "sir"? *(Earl moves to Ray, holding his finger up.)*

EARL. Look, pal —

RAY. Go ahead, Earl. Poke me in the chest. I need to get poked again. Real hard. Right here! *(Ray pokes his own chest, daring Earl. Pause. Earl glares at him as Esteban stands by.)* Come on, Earl. It's been a long time, hasn't it? *(Pause with the brothers staring each other down as Esteban watches. Earl backs down and turns away from Ray.)*

EARL. Look — Let's just relax here, all right? How 'bout we just relax?

RAY. I am relaxed. "Pal." *(Earl moves to table, sits and pours himself a drink. Esteban keeps staring at Ray.)*

EARL. *(At table.)* No need to get all worked up over nothing. Things are hard enough. You gotta be careful at a time like this. I mean — How 'bout we just have a — have a drink.

RAY. He doesn't drink, remember? He *pretends* to drink. He's a pretender.

EARL. Back off, Ray! What kind of bug have you got up your ass anyway? Huh? The man comes over here with *soup*. He comes over here just as polite and neighborly as he can be and you jump all over him like a cold sweat. What is the matter with you?

24

RAY. Tell him to stop staring at me.

EARL. You've terrified him is what you've done.

RAY. Tell him to stop staring at me.

EARL. Come on, Esteban — *(Moves toward Esteban.)* Look — I apologize for my brother's behavior —

RAY. Don't apologize for me! I don't need you to apologize for my behavior! Tell him to stop staring at me. *(Earl escorts Esteban back to table and sits him down.)*

EARL. Everything's fine. Don't pay any attention to him. He — flies off the handle like this — I don't know. He — it'll be all right. Everything's fine. *(Earl sits Esteban down, then sits in the other chair. Pause.)*

RAY. *(Mimicking Earl.)* "Everything's fine." *(Pause. Ray stares at them. Esteban sticks his finger in the soup.)*

EARL. Everything's fine, Esteban.

RAY. Stop saying that! Stop saying that over and over again like some lame prayer! Everything's *not* fine! Everything's the opposite of "fine"! "Fine" is when your heart soars! When you're in love or something. That's when things are "fine." Right, Esteban? "Fine" is — *(Ray suddenly stops. Long pause. Earl and Esteban stare at him.)* I wanna know about this woman.

EARL. What woman?

RAY. This woman — This mysterious woman: "Conchalla," "Conchita," whatever her name is.

ESTEBAN. "Conchita." *(Esteban starts giggling uncontrollably. Short pause.)*

RAY. Shut up! You shut up! *(Esteban stops abruptly. Short pause.)* Who is she, Earl?

EARL. His girlfriend. Henry's girlfriend.

RAY. Well, see now that — just confuses the hell outta me. I never even knew Henry had a girlfriend.

EARL. I told you he had a girlfriend.

RAY. You told me jack shit, Earl.

EARL. I told you on the phone.

RAY. How long's he had this "girlfriend"? Where'd he meet her?

EARL. I don't know where he met her. *(Pause.)*

RAY. Where'd he meet her, Esteban?

ESTEBAN. In jail.

RAY. In jail. That's cute. *(He turns to Earl.)*

EARL. I never met the woman, myself.

RAY. *You* never met her but Esteban here knows all about her evidently.

EARL. I heard he had a girlfriend but I never actually laid eyes on her.

ESTEBAN. They meet in jail.

RAY. What do they have, a coeducational drunk tank down here in Bernalillo?

ESTEBAN. They meet in jail.

RAY. That where you met her too?

EARL. Don't get personal.

RAY. Well, this is kind of a personal thing here, Earl. Girlfriends and jail. This is something different than a photograph from 1931. This is something actual here.

EARL. The man's a neighbor!

RAY. Yeah, right. Come here, neighbor! I wanna show you something. *(Ray grabs Esteban by the back of the neck, hauls him out of the chair and starts taking him toward Henry's corpse. Earl leaps up.)*

EARL. What're you doing! *(Earl grabs ahold of Esteban's arm and pulls against Ray.)*

RAY. Come here. Now take a look at this.

EARL. Ray! *(Ray manages to swing Esteban upstage at the head of the bed with Earl still holding onto him. Ray is downstage of the bed, back to audience. He whips the sheet and blanket back, revealing Henry's face to Esteban but blocking it from view of the audience. Esteban stares at the corpse.)*

RAY. Go ahead — Touch his face, Esteban! This is Henry. "Mr. Henry"! The man you've been bringing soup to for all these years. *(Ray grabs Esteban's hand and pushes it down onto the face of the corpse. Earl tries to pull Esteban away, but it's too late. Holding Esteban's hand down on corpse:)* You feel how cold that is? Like ice! Like stone in a river. Does that look like a man who's ever gonna eat another bowl of soup? *(Ray releases Esteban's hand and spreads the blanket back over the corpse, covering the head completely. Esteban just stands there in shock, trembling. Earl moves slowly back toward table. Pause.)* So —

EARL. *(Moving toward table.)* You better get outta here, Ray.

RAY. I just got here, Earl.

EARL. There's a certain — kind of cruelty to you, isn't there? I never realized that before.

RAY. Yeah, I get mean as a snake when I don't see the whole picture.

EARL. *(Referring to Esteban.)* You had no call to be doing that to him.

RAY. What're we gonna do? Pretend?

EARL. You come waltzing in here — No idea — No concept whatsoever.

RAY. Concept? *(Earl sits at table. Esteban begins to softly weep upstage.)*

EARL. Yeah. Yeah, that's right. No concept that there might be repercussions. That there might be consequences — serious consequences.

RAY. *(Moving toward Earl.)* Have you lost your tiny mind out here, Earl? Is that what happened to you? Sitting here all alone with dead Daddy for days on end. Something went on here! Didn't it, Earl? Something I'm not being let in on!

EARL. Nothing went on!

RAY. "Nothing went on." "Everything's fine." *(Moves in closer to Earl.)* Henry was tough as an old boot! You know that. He could kill two pints and a six-pack in one sitting and never skip a beat! Now you want me to believe he takes off on a two-day binge with some Indian chippie and drops dead overnight? Is that what you're telling me?

EARL. *(Smashes down on table.)* It was an accumulating illness! He was a fuckin' alcoholic, Ray! *(Long pause. Just the sound of Esteban softly weeping.)*

RAY. *(To Esteban.)* Stop that goddamn whimpering! *(Esteban stops.)* You weren't related to him, were you? *(Esteban shakes his head, stands there trembling by Henry's bed.)* Then what're you carrying on about? I'm his *son!* You don't see me whimpering do you? *(Esteban shakes his head.)* I've got every right to be whimpering but you don't see me doing that.

EARL. Ah, Ray, give it up.

RAY. *(Turning on Earl.)* Or you! What about you? I suppose you think you've got some sort of private thing going — some kind of special link to the corpse or something. You're in deep commun-

27

ion here with old Henry. *(Pause.)* Old dead Henry. *(Pause.)*
EARL. What'd you ever come out here for, Ray? Why'd you even
bother?
RAY. I just couldn't believe it, I guess.
EARL. You thought he'd live forever? Is that it?
RAY. No. I just thought —
EARL. What?
RAY. Maybe I'd see him one more time. Alive.
EARL. Yeah. You thought maybe you'd get to the bottom of
something — clear things up? Make some big reconciliation.
RAY. I don't need any reconciliation! I don't need it with you either!
EARL. Good. That's good, Ray — because, guess what? It'll never
happen. He's gone now. *(Earl moves away from Ray to Esteban. He
puts his arm around Esteban's shoulder and pats him, then starts lead-
ing him toward door.)*
RAY. What're you doing?
EARL. We're gonna go down and make that phone call, Ray.
Down to the Sonic there.
RAY. What phone call? The meat-wagon boys? So — your little
period of mourning has suddenly come to an end?
EARL. Let it go, Ray! Give it up! Go on back to wherever you
came from. *(Pause.)*
RAY. No — No, I'm not gonna give it up, Earl. You know why?
Because I'm your witness. I'm your little brother. I saw you, Earl.
I saw the whole thing.
EARL. You saw shit.
RAY. I saw you! *(Earl takes Esteban toward door.)*
EARL. Come on, Esteban.
RAY. I saw you run! *(Earl suddenly whirls around and attacks Ray.
He overpowers him and sends him crashing across stage into refrigera-
tor. Ray hits the floor. Earl crosses to him and kicks Ray in the stom-
ach. Ray collapses. Esteban stays by door, watching. Pause as Earl
straightens out his coat, then turns back to Esteban. Ray stays on floor.)*
EARL. I'm sorry about all this, Esteban. I truly am. I hate this
kind of thing, myself. Family stuff. *(Earl moves toward Esteban,
then stops about halfway. He looks back at Ray, then says to Esteban:)*
I had no idea my brother was so screwed up in the head like this.
I mean I knew he had some problems but I thought he'd pulled

himself back together. Otherwise I'd never have called him. Anyhow — we better go make that call. *(Earl goes to door and opens it for Esteban. Esteban exits, then Earl turns back to Ray. To Ray, on floor:)* Well — At least this'll give you a chance to spend a little time alone with Henry, Ray. Maybe that's what you need. Did me a world of good. *(Earl exits, closes door behind him. Pause. Ray stares at door, then hauls himself to his feet, holding his ribs. He stares at Henry's corpse, then crosses to bed and stops with his back to audience. Pause as he stares down at corpse; then, with a quick jerk, he draws the curtain closed in front of the bed. Short pause, then lights fade quickly to black.)*

End of Act One

PRELUDE TO ACT TWO
(DRUNKEN RHUMBA)

Lights go to black. A new, more spirited mariachi piece comes up to volume. White spotlight hits Henry and Conchalla on the opposite side of the stage (extreme down right). They are still amazingly drunk and in the same tight embrace. Again they dance across the apron, doing some variations and disappear off left. Spotlight out; lights up on set to begin Act Two.

ACT TWO

Scene: Day. Same set. The sound of rubber gloves snapping in the dark; labored breathing. Lights come up on two funeral attendants dressed in gray suits, rubber gloves, and white gauze masks covering nose and mouth. They are struggling to place Henry's corpse inside a black canvas body bag. A stretcher sits on the floor downstage of the bed. They are having a great deal of difficulty getting the body to fit into the bag. They work nervously, under the constant scrutiny of Ray, who sits in the stage left chair. Taxi, a cab driver from Albuquerque, stands upstage of the table facing audience. He is drinking from a bottle of Tiger Rose and fiddling with the tools in Henry's toolbox, which is still on the table. The photo album lies open on the table where Earl left it. Ray continues to focus on the funeral attendants as Taxi rambles on.

TAXI. *(To Ray.)* Hey, look — for a hundred bucks and a bottle of Tiger Rose — are you kidding? This is gravy! This is a day off for

me. I'll just regard it as that. A whole free day, thanks to you. Whatever your name is. I didn't catch the name — *(Taxi toasts Ray with the bottle but Ray ignores him. Attendants continue struggling with body.)* I mean, all the dispatcher told me is, some guy from Bernalillo wanted to talk to me. That's all the information I got. *(Pause.)* Oh, well — I was on the verge of quitting anyhow, if you wanna know the truth. Company sucks. All they care about is the damn meter. Human interest is not number one on their list. Far as they're concerned they'd just as soon have a damn robot drive the cars. Cut their insurance in half. It's coming to that. I guarandamn-teeya. Computerized robot taxis. You won't even see a human being behind the wheel anymore. I'm not lyin'. *(Pause. Attendants keep working, making some progress, trying to zip the bag shut. Ray keeps watching them intently. Taxi drinks and picks up the large ratchet out of the toolbox; the same ratchet Ray was handling in Act One. He starts fooling with it as he talks, causing the ratchet to make a rhythmic click-ing.)* Oh, well — Thank God I'm self-sufficient. I could head on out to Norman, Oklahoma, and get me a job easy. Plenty a cabs out there. College town too. Plenty a babes. A whole slam a Miss Oklahoma's have come outta Norman, lemme tell ya. I ain't lyin'. You wouldn't believe the types. Legs up to here. Asses like hard can-taloupes. Some gorgeous babes in that country. No question. I could head on out there and be in high cotton. *(Pause. Taxi keeps clicking the ratchet. Ray keeps staring at attendants as they work.)* Nice ratchet.
RAY. Don't mess with that.
TAXI. What?
RAY. I said, don't mess with that.
TAXI. Oh. Sorry. *(Taxi puts ratchet back in toolbox; takes another swig.)*
RAY. That doesn't belong to you.
TAXI. No — I know. I was just uh — admiring it, that's all. *(Pause. Attendants keep working.)* Were these your daddy's tools?
RAY. They're mine.
TAXI. Oh. Pretty nice. Cheap but nice. *(Taxi idly shifts to the album and starts leafing through it.)*
RAY. *(Focused on attendants.)* Don't mess with that either.
TAXI. Okay. Sorry. Just — Just lookin' that's all.
RAY. Well, don't look. It's none of your business.

31

TAXI. Right. *(Pause.)* Well — Like I was saying about uh — Norman.
RAY. Who's Norman?
TAXI. No — I mean, uh — Norman, Oklahoma. You know —
Like I was saying before about Norman, Oklahoma.
RAY. What about it?
TAXI. Well — I mean, that's what I was saying — I can go on
out there and if the taxi deal doesn't work out I can always get in
on the midnight pizza delivery thing. You know — Late-night
stuff. I've heard all about it, believe you me. Two, three in the
morning sometimes, you can get a delivery call. Take a pineapple
combo over to some dormitory, for instance. Well — you know
who orders a pineapple combo, don't ya? *(Pause. Ray doesn't look at
him; keeps watching attendants.)*
RAY. What?
TAXI. I said, you know who usually orders a pineapple combo,
don't ya? Girls! That's who always orders those pineapple combos.
Girls mostly. So there you are in the perfect setup! Standing there
on the front stoop, ringing the bell with red pizza juice dripping
down your elbow. And who comes to the door but the goddamn
Miss America contest! *(Henry's body, now encased in the bag, suddenly crashes to the floor as the attendants lose their grip. Ray stands
abruptly. Everyone freezes. Pause.)*
RAY. That's my father you just dropped. That's not a piece of lug-
gage or a sack of feed! That's my father. Get out. Get outta here.
(Attendants exit.)
TAXI. They don't care. They're just hauling stiffs. They've seen it
a thousand times. A corpse is a corpse. Might as well be roadkill
to them.
RAY. Shut up.
TAXI. You need some help with that? *(Ray motions "no." Goes to
door and calls back the attendants.)*
RAY. You guys come back. Both of you come back in here.
*(Attendants reenter and lift Henry's body again, struggling with the
weight as Ray slowly closes in on them. Taxi stays where he is.)* You
aren't the type of creeps who make sick jokes behind other people's backs are you? Because if you are I'll find out about it and
I'll seek vengeance on your heads. *(Pause.)* Now get outta here.
(The attendants hustle the corpse out the door and disappear. Ray

stays in open doorway looking offstage, after them. Taxi stays at the table with album.)
TAXI. *(Laughing, still going through album.)* That's good! That's good! "I'll seek vengeance on your heads!" That's a good one. Where'd you come up with that? I'll have to remember that. I can use that. That has a kinda — old-fashioned ring to it. You know, like — King Arthur or something? Remember him? *(Ray closes door and turns to Taxi. Pause. They stare at each other.)*
RAY. What'd I tell you about that album?
TAXI. What? *(He quickly looks back at album.)* Oh — *(He shuts album.)* Sorry. I forgot. *(Pause. Ray moves to Henry's empty bed. He stares at bed, then smooths the blanket and sheet. He draws the curtain closed in front of bed and just stands there staring at curtain with his back to Taxi. Pause. Stays by table.)* Well — Anyhow, I appreciate the hundred bucks and the Tiger Rose. I surely do. Came as a complete surprise to me when the dispatcher gave me the message. Not that I don't deserve it. *(Laughs.)* I deserve every bit of it. You better believe it! *(Pause. Ray doesn't move, just keeps staring at bed with his back to Taxi.)* How'd you track me down, anyhow? That's a big mystery. I couldn't figure that one out. I mean it's been almost a week ago I was out here. Least a week, wasn't it? I lose track. *(Pause. Ray doesn't move. Silence.)* Well, anyhow, I suppose this is a hard time for you, huh? I mean, I don't mind answering any questions you might have. You said you had some questions. Not that I could tell you much — *(Pause. Ray turns to him and stares, then moves downstage to table and sits; pours himself a drink. Taxi slowly pulls out a chair, as though to sit down at the table.)*
RAY. *(Cold.)* Don't sit down at this table. *(Taxi freezes, then stands and pushes chair back in place. Pause.)* I don't know you well enough for you to be sitting at this table.
TAXI. Right — Uh — Sorry. I was thinking maybe if I sat at the table — we could uh — we could get to know each other — a little — maybe. You know — break the ice. *(Laughs.)*
RAY. What makes you think I want to get to know you? I didn't pay you to come all the way out here so I could get to know you. What do you think you are?
TAXI. Me? Well — I'm —
RAY. Go over and stand by the door.

TAXI. What? *(Pause. Taxi looks toward door, then back to Ray, but doesn't move.)*

RAY. *(Pointing to door.)* Over there. *(Taxi looks to door again, then back to Ray.)*

TAXI. Now, you mean?

RAY. Yeah. Now. When you're a stranger in somebody's house, you don't automatically assume you can sit down at their table and fool around aimlessly with their father's possessions.

TAXI. I thought they were yours. You told me —

RAY. Go over and stand by the door! *(Taxi looks at door again, then back to Ray. Pause, then he crosses to door, taking his bottle with him, and stands there. He stares at Ray.)*

TAXI. Right here?

RAY. A little to your right. *(Taxi adjusts his position slightly.)*

TAXI. How's this?

RAY. That's good. Now stay right there. Okay?

TAXI. Okay. *(Takes a drink from his bottle.)* Sure. You bet.

RAY. Don't move from that spot.

TAXI. Okay.

RAY. See if you can manage that. Now, just for a minute, try to avoid thinking of yourself as anything special. All right? Anything out of the ordinary. You're nothing. Just like me. An empty nothing. A couple of nothings whose lives have never amounted to anything and never will. Do you think you can go along with this?

TAXI. Well, I don't know. I mean — it's not exactly the way I was raised. My uncle used to —

RAY. I'm not interested in the way you were raised, or your uncle.

TAXI. Right.

RAY. I'm not interested in Norman, Oklahoma, or "babes" or pizza juice dripping down your arm or your employment problems either.

TAXI. Right.

RAY. I'm only interested in one thing.

TAXI. *(Pause.)* What's that?

RAY. What happened that night you showed up here in your cab to take my father out to go fishing? What exactly happened? *(Pause.)*

TAXI. Oh. Well — I don't know. Nothin' special. I mean, I got

34

the call. You know, it was kinda unusual but — *(Taxi starts to move toward Ray.)*

RAY. Just stay by the door! *(Taxi freezes, then returns to his spot by the door. Pause. He takes another drink from his bottle.)*

TAXI. Right here?

RAY. A little to your left. *(Taxi adjusts his position.)*

RAY. That's fine. Now — You were saying — It was unusual?

TAXI. Yeah.

RAY. Kind of unusual but not all that unusual.

TAXI. *(Stays put.)* No, right. I mean — we get calls now and then from folks way out in the boondocks like this. This is big country — Lotta ground between places. Folks need a ride. Stranded folks. I mean, I remember as a kid we grew up a hundred and twenty miles from the nearest drive-in.

RAY. Don't get off the subject. *(Pause.)*

TAXI. What?

RAY. Your mind is wandering. Don't allow it to do that.

TAXI. Oh — Yeah — Well — like I was saying — all I do is drive 'em to the nearest movie. Forty, fifty miles maybe sometimes. Just to see Clint Eastwood.

RAY. You arrived here at the house! Right? I don't care how long it took you to get here. You arrived. Now, what was going on here at the house when you arrived?

TAXI. Here?

RAY. Yeah. That's right. Here.

TAXI. Oh. Well — nothing really. I mean — I remember knocking. I remember this feeling like — maybe I was at the wrong house or something.

RAY. Why was that? *(Lights slowly shift. A glowing amber light comes up on the curtain in front of Henry's bed. At the same time the lights on the rest of the stage dim to a pale moonlit glow.)*

TAXI. Well, I mean — there wasn't any answer at the door. I kept knocking and — *(Taxi moves slowly toward the curtain and the bed as Ray turns slowly in his chair until he's directly facing the audience. Ray stays in this position, looking directly out at audience through the entire flashback. As he crosses to curtain in front of bed:)* I could hear something from inside so I knew there was somebody in here. I kept knocking but all I heard was this moaning like — this weep-

35

ing. I didn't know what to make of it. Door was open so — I just let myself in. And there he was — lying on his side in bed there. Sobbing like — *(The curtain opens slowly on its own, revealing the living Henry, lying on his belly, softly weeping. Taxi approaches him. To Henry:)* Mr. Moss? *(Pause.)* Mr. Moss? *(Henry suddenly sits up on the edge of the bed with a jerk and stares blankly at Taxi. He stops weeping. Pause. He gets up fast and snatches the bottle of Tiger Rose away from Taxi, then crosses to the door, staggering slightly.)*

HENRY. *(Crossing to door.)* The hell you doin' with my bottle! The fuck is this? Time is it, anyway? *(Henry opens the door, looks out, then slams it shut. He turns to Taxi and stares at him.)*

TAXI. Did you — call a cab, Mr. Moss?

HENRY. A what?

TAXI. A taxi. From Albuquerque? Verde Cabs?

HENRY. Taxi? The fuck is this? A taxi from Albuquerque?

TAXI. Somebody called a cab.

HENRY. Somebody?

TAXI. Somebody must have.

HENRY. What if they did? Maybe they did, maybe they didn't. What's the big deal? *(Henry crosses to table and sits in upstage chair, ignoring Ray, as though Ray didn't exist. Henry drinks from Taxi's bottle. Looking at bottle.)* The fuck is this junk? *(Pushes bottle on table.)* Where'd this come from?

TAXI. I'm the taxi.

HENRY. What?

TAXI. I'm the taxi from Albuquerque.

HENRY. *(Laughs.)* You're the taxi? That's something! You look like a damn taxi. You got that yellow stripe down your back. *(He grabs bottle back and drinks, then gags on it.)* What the hell is this stuff anyhow?

TAXI. Tiger Rose.

HENRY. Stuff stinks! *(Pushes bottle away again.)* That's not my stuff. Where the hell's my stuff? *(Henry stands and starts wandering around looking for his bottle.)*

TAXI. Did you wanna go somewhere, Mr. Moss? Did you want me to take you somewhere?

HENRY. *(Searching.)* I had a bottle here. You didn't walk off with my damn bottle did ya?

TAXI. No, sir, I just got here.

HENRY. Well, somebody's got my bottle!

TAXI. Mr. Moss, did you need me to take you somewhere? That's what I'm here for. I'm here to take you wherever you want to go.

HENRY. *(Stops, looks at Taxi.)* You're here to take me?

TAXI. That's right.

HENRY. Where do I wanna go?

TAXI. Well — That's what I'm here to find out — I mean —

HENRY. Where could it be that I wanna go?

TAXI. I have no idea, sir.

HENRY. What the hell happened to that bottle! *(Henry starts searching for bottle again.)*

TAXI. Maybe that was it, huh? Maybe you needed me to take you to get a bottle?

HENRY. That's what you think. That's probably what you think! Do I look that desperate to you?

TAXI. No, sir.

HENRY. You lyin' sack a doggy doo-doo.

TAXI. I'm going to have to go, Mr. Moss. *(Taxi makes a move to leave. Henry stops him.)*

HENRY. Just a second, just a second, just a second! Just hold on here. You're the taxi, right?

TAXI. That's right. Yeah.

HENRY. And you've got a mission. Is that it? You were called to come here?

TAXI. Yes, sir.

HENRY. So somebody musta called you out here. Is that correct?

TAXI. Yeah. That's correct.

HENRY. And you think that was me who called you out here?

TAXI. Well — I don't know who it was but —

HENRY. Well, it was me. Why beat around the bush about it?

TAXI. It was you?

HENRY. 'Course it was. You don't see anybody else around here, do ya?

TAXI. Well, I'm ready, Mr. Moss.

HENRY. Yeah, yeah, yeah. You're ready. You're ready. Sure. You're always ready. Suppose you got the meter runnin' out there too, huh? Rackin' it up for air time! Click-clocking away!

TAXI. Well, the company says you gotta —

HENRY. Fuck the company, all right! Fuck the company right where it fits. What're you, a company man? Is that what you are?

TAXI. No, sir, I'm —

HENRY. Are you a company man or are you your own man? That's the question. What is it? You can't have it both ways.

TAXI. I'm my own —

HENRY. You don't have a clue, buster.

TAXI. I just need some kind of insurance that you actually want the cab —

HENRY. Insurance! Money, you mean? Cash money? That's what you're worried about?

TAXI. No, I — *(Henry starts digging cash out of his pockets. He crosses to table and slams it down.)*

HENRY. Cash money! Mean green! How 'bout that! Look at that! Where would a desperate man come up with so much cash! Surprised ya, huh? Give ya a start?

TAXI. No, sir.

HENRY. That's blood money right there, Mr. Taxi! World War II blood money! Guess how many dead Japs that cost? Take a guess.

TAXI. I, uh —

HENRY. Beyond your imagination, bud. Beyond your imagination.

TAXI. Well, I didn't think you didn't have any money, Mr. Moss. That wasn't what I meant.

HENRY. You got any women, Taxi? *(Pause. Taxi stares at him.)*

TAXI. Women? You mean —

HENRY. I mean, women. The female kind.

TAXI. Well, I've got a girlfriend, if that's what you mean.

HENRY. Girlfriend? Don't gimme that shit. "Girlfriend." I mean women. Women women. Real women!

TAXI. Well — she's real, all right.

HENRY. I got one. I got a doozy. Make yer tail swim, Taxi. Know what she did to me? You wanna know? Guess. Bet you'll never guess.

TAXI. Mr. Moss, I gotta —

HENRY. She pronounced me dead! That's what she did. *(Pause.)*

TAXI. Dead?

HENRY. That's it. Dead. Ever heard of such a thing? That's what she did to me. Can you imagine? Right in jail too. In front of every-

one. We were both incarcerated together and she made that pro-nouncement. Publicly! Standing right over my semiconscious body. She just bellowed it out to the general jail community at large. "Señor Moss is dead!" Now it's all over town. All over this territory. Everyone thinks I'm dead! *(Pause. Henry grabs bottle again; drinks. Taxi just stands there.)*
TAXI. Well — They must know she was lying by now, don't they?
HENRY. On the contrary! Nobody thinks she was lying. Not a single solitary soul.
TAXI. Well — I mean — You're not dead, so —
HENRY. You think I'm not dead. That's you. But you're not from around here, are you?
TAXI. No, sir, but —
HENRY. You're from Albuquerque.
TAXI. Yes, sir.
HENRY. So what difference does it make what you think? I'm talkin' about the ones right around here. The real ones. They're all that count. All the local ones. I'm a well-known figure around here, in case you didn't know that, buster. They all think I'm dead now on account a her.
TAXI. Well, don't they see you walking around and talking and everything?
HENRY. Walking around and talking? What the hell difference does that make? There's a whole shitload of "walkers" and "talkers" — fabricating and perambulating their butts off! You think they're all in the land of the living? Is that what you think? Huh?
TAXI. I know, but usually —
HENRY. Usually nothin'! There's nothin' usual about this! I'm in a serious jam on account of this woman! She's trying to obliterate me before my natural time! She took out an obituary in the paper. "Henry Jamison Moss; Dead. Deceased. Causes unknown." She did that to me.
TAXI. Well, can't you just explain to everyone that she was mis-taken?
HENRY. What's the situation look like to you, bub? Do I look like a dead man or what?
TAXI. No, sir.
HENRY. Not the least bit, huh? Not around the eyes a little?

39

Look around the eyes. That's what gives it away. Look closely here. Come over and give it a good hard look-see. *(Taxi reluctantly approaches Henry and stops in front of him, staring hard at Henry's eyes.)* No, you've got to get in here close! Scrutinize this. Penetrate past the outer covering. *(Taxi moves in closer and bends in toward Henry's face, staring hard at his eyes. Henry opens his eyes wide, using his fingers and thumbs to pry them open.)* Now — Look right deep into the pupil, where it's dark. Where it drops off into nowhere. You see that? Right straight in there like you were riding a train into a black tunnel. What do you see? Tell me what you see. *(Pause. Taxi stares hard into Henry's eyes.)*

TAXI. Nothing. *(Henry drops his hands from his eyes.)*

HENRY. Exactly! Exactly my point. Absolutely nothing!

TAXI. No, I mean, they look okay to me.

HENRY. They look dead!

TAXI. No, sir —

HENRY. Don't jerk my chain, Taxi-man! You're a lyin' dog! Yer from Albuquerque! *(Taxi backs off from Henry.)*

TAXI. Are you ready to go someplace, Mr. Moss, because — I've gotta head on back if you don't need the cab. *(Henry moves in front of him fast and stops him.)*

HENRY. Not so fast, not so fast, not so fast!

TAXI. I can't be just — hanging around here, Mr. Moss. There's other customers waiting. *(Pause. Henry pats Taxi on the shoulder.)*

HENRY. So — Just from your — casual observation, you think there might be a little spark inside there, huh? *(Pointing to his eyes.)* A little ember of hope?

TAXI. You're not dead, all right! As far as I can tell you are not dead! *(Pause.)*

HENRY. Good, that's good. That's the first positive note I've heard in months. Tell ya what we're gonna do — Tell ya what, Taxi. Here's what we're gonna do — Ya like to trout fish?

TAXI. Well — sure. Haven't done it in a while, but —

HENRY. Well, that's what we're gonna do, then. Conchalla likes to trout fish too. We're gonna go pick her up and hit the river. You can take it up with her.

TAXI. Conchalla?

HENRY. That's right. Conchalla Lupina. That's the woman. The woman I was referring to. You can take the whole issue up with her out on the Pecos. *(Henry grabs Taxi by the shoulder and starts to weave toward the door.)*

TAXI. What issue?

HENRY. The question of my being! My aliveness! My actuality in this world! Whether or not I'm dead or not! What the hell've we been talkin' about here? Pay attention to the subject!

TAXI. But, I'm not —

HENRY. Just get that cab fired up, bub! Get those pistons rockin'! You'll see. Conchalla's a very influential woman around here. Sharp as jailhouse coffee. You can have it out with her, toe to toe. You can argue my case for me. I've got no one else. Couple a lamebrain sons who couldn't find their peckers in a pickle jar. Take hold of my arm now, boy. Take ahold! *(Taxi grabs Henry's arm.)* That feel like a living arm to you?

TAXI. Yes, sir. It does.

HENRY. Attaboy! You tell her that for me. She might just listen to an outsider from Albuquerque. She might just listen. *(Henry staggers out through door and disappears, leaving Taxi behind. Taxi closes door and turns to face Ray, who remains seated, facing audience. Lights return to previous setup. Ray takes a drink. Pause. He keeps staring out at audience with his back to Taxi.)*

RAY. That's it? That's all you can remember?

TAXI. *(Stays by door.)* That's pretty much it. Yeah.

RAY. No more details?

TAXI. Details? Like what?

RAY. Are you still on your spot? Your same spot?

TAXI. What spot?

RAY. Your spot by the door where I told you to stay.

TAXI. *(Adjusting.)* Oh — Yeah. Yeah, I'm still there. *(Taxi jumps into position. Pause.)*

RAY. Good. That's very good. *(Pause. Ray gets up from chair and crosses to Henry's bed. He sits on bed, facing audience. Pause.)*

TAXI. Look — why don't I just give you the hundred bucks back, okay? *(He digs in his pocket and pulls out money.)* I'll keep the Tiger Rose and we'll call it even-steven. Just for the trip out here. Gas and time involved. We'll write that off. How's that sound?

RAY. *(Laughs.)* "Even-steven"? *(Pause. Ray goes silent. Taxi moves*

41

very cautiously toward Ray, holding out the money to him.)
TAXI. That sound fair to you? I mean — I don't think this is gonna work out, personally. I just got a feeling — I mean, I had a whole different idea about this. Here. *(Offering money to Ray.)* How about it?
RAY. You keep that money, Taxi-man. That's your money. You put it back in your pocket. I don't want it. You put it in your pocket and go back to the door, like I told you, and stay there. All right?
TAXI. Oh no —
RAY. Go back to the door. *(Pause. Taxi slowly puts money back in his pocket, returns to his spot by the door and stands there. He stares at Ray, trembling slightly. Pause. Ray stares out.)*
TAXI. Thing I'm gonna do is go back to Texas. Never shoulda left Texas in the first place. That's the whole problem, right there. I don't fit up here in this country. You get raised up in a friendly place, you think the whole rest of the world's just as friendly. Boy, are you sadly mistaken. *(Ray stands slowly from bed and moves to refrigerator. Taxi stays.)*
RAY. You're not from Texas. You're from Albuquerque.
TAXI. I'm originally from Texas. Tyler, Texas — born and raised. *(Ray opens refrigerator and stares into it.)*
RAY. Texans don't whine. No whiners down in Texas. They kicked 'em all out.
TAXI. What do you know about it? My great-great-grandmother was slaughtered by Comanches. I guess that makes me from Texas, all right.
RAY. *(Looking in fridge.)* Your great-great-grandmother?
TAXI. That's right.
RAY. Your great-great-grandmother was slaughtered by Comanches? Sounds like a story to me.
TAXI. A story?
RAY. A fabrication, passed down from one generation to another. Sounds like that kind of a story. A prideful story.
TAXI. Prideful? There's nothin' prideful about being slaughtered. *(Ray takes out the jar of jalapeños and slams refrigerator door shut. He opens jar, takes out a pepper, pops it in his mouth, then crosses slowly toward Taxi with the jar. Taxi stays.)*
RAY. *(Slowly crossing to Taxi.)* Thing about that kind of a story,

Taxi-man, is that the very first fabricator — the original liar who started this little rumor about your slaughtered great-great-grandma — he's dead and gone now, right? Vanished from this earth! All the ones who knew him are dead and gone. All that's left is a cracked tintype, maybe; a gnarly lock of bloody hair; some fingernail clippings in a leather pouch. So there's really no way to verify this little story of yours, is there? This little history. *(Pause. Ray stops very close to Taxi's face, chewing on the pepper.)*

TAXI. You're not calling me a liar, are you?

RAY. Your whole family's a pack of liars. They were born liars. They couldn't help themselves. That's why it's important to try to get at the heart of things, don't you think? Somebody, somewhere along the line has to try to get at the heart of things. *(Pause. They stare at each other, then Ray offers jar of peppers out to Taxi.)* Jalapeño?

TAXI. No. Thank you.

RAY. Come on, now! You're from Texas! You can take a little heat. *(Ray slowly takes out a Jalapeño and pushes it into Taxi's mouth. Taxi chews. Ray moves away from him to table and sits. Taxi starts quietly choking on pepper, eyes watering, breaking out in a sweat. He wants to grab the bottle off the table to cool the fire but is afraid to move from his spot. Seated at table:)* No way to verify this story at all. It's like my brother. Just like my brother. He's a fabricator too. He makes something up out of thin air, thinking I'll fall for it. Just swallow it whole. No questions. "Dad's dead." That's how he put it. "Dad's dead." Simple as that. End of issue.

TAXI. *(Choking, gasping for air.)* Could — Could I — Could I get my bottle, please? Do you think — *(Pause. Ray stares at him as he chokes, then slides bottle in Taxi's direction. Taxi hesitates to leave his spot, but Ray gestures for him to go ahead and take bottle. Taxi lunges for bottle, takes a huge swig, clears his throat and stares at Ray, his eyes popping from the heat.)* Thanks.

RAY. You go back over to your spot now, Taxi.

TAXI. Oh, no — Couldn't we — just be friendly?

RAY. You just go on back over there. You remember where it is, don't you?

TAXI. What? My — my — spot?

RAY. Yeah. *(Pause. Taxi moves back to his spot by door; turns to Ray.)*

TAXI. Was this it?

RAY. Close enough.

TAXI. Look — I've got this terrible feeling all of a sudden. I — I mean I — I don't know anything. I didn't think there was anything wrong here to begin with. I mean when I first came over, you know. I wouldn't have volunteered for this if I thought there was anything wrong here. I just — I don't — I gotta go now. I really gotta go — *(Taxi moves to door as though to exit. Ray suddenly flies at him from the chair and pins him up against the door. Ray grabs him by the chest. Taxi offers no resistance, just whimpers.)*

RAY. *(Close to Taxi's face.)* I didn't give you a hundred bucks and a bottle of Tiger Rose so you could skip out on me! What'd you think this was, a free ride? Huh! Is that what you thought?

TAXI. I don't want the hundred bucks! I told you that!

RAY. You took it! It's too late now. You owe me. You're in debt to me. You're deeply in debt!

TAXI. Oh, my God! Oh, my God in heaven. *(Pause. Ray lets go of him and backs off slowly but stands near him. Taxi slumps back against door; his head bows like he's on the verge of breaking down. He trembles all over.)* I need to get back and see my girlfriend!

RAY. You don't have a girlfriend.

TAXI. I do! I do too! I do so have a girlfriend! I'm from Texas and I've got a girlfriend! How come you're trying to take everything away from me? I don't wanna be here! I don't wanna be here at all! I want — I wanna leave now! I wanna go!

RAY. Yeah, but you owe me something now, Taxi. You owe me a little story.

TAXI. What story?

RAY. The story of when you all returned; the returning story. When you came back here. To this place, right here. With my dad and this woman and a string of fish. *(Short pause, then Conchalla bursts through the door, knocking Taxi toward the bed. Henry stumbles through, close behind her, holding up a very small fish by the tail. Ray moves extreme downstage right and stands, facing audience throughout flashback. The other characters ignore him. Taxi falls in with Henry and Conchalla as an active member of the flashback. Conchalla is extremely drunk and singing loudly in some strange dialect that sounds like a mixture of Spanish and Indian. She carries a bottle of tequila and heads straight for the tub, pushing Taxi out of*

44

*her way. She turns the hot water on full blast and starts taking her
skirt and blouse off as she continues to sing. Henry stumbles to the
table, as drunk as Conchalla, and flops the fish down on it. He picks
the fish up and starts flopping it back and forth on the table as he sings
in competition with Conchalla.)*
HENRY. *(Singing loudly:)*
   Gonna tie my pecker to a tree, to a tree
   Gonna tie my pecker to a tree
   Gonna tie my pecker to a tree, to a tree
   Gonna tie my pecker to a tree.
*(Pause as Henry looks around the room, ignoring Ray. Conchalla goes
into humming her song and continues getting ready for her bath. She
drinks from bottle and takes some kind of oil out of her belt and starts
oiling her skin as the water steams in the tub. Taxi looks on.)* Look at
this fish! Now, that's a fish! *(Henry holds the tiny fish up as though
it were a trophy. Conchalla laughs.)*
CONCHALLA. That is no fish! That is a fish wishing to become
a fish. A wish fish!
HENRY. *(Turning toward Conchalla, weaving.)* I knew — I just
knew — Now, how did I know that you were gonna rain on my
rainbow like that? How'd I know that?
CONCHALLA. That is a minnow! That is a bait fish, maybe.
HENRY. *(Holding up fish.)* That's a legitimate fish right there!
Wouldn't you say that was a legitimate fish, Taxi? That's a fish!
TAXI. Well, yeah — it's a fish but — you probably shoulda let
him grow some.
HENRY. Let him grow? What the hell good's that? Let him grow!
Ya mean throw him back is what ya mean. That's what ya mean,
isn't it? Throw him back. *(To Conchalla.)* He wants me to throw
back my catch of the day.
CONCHALLA. That is no fish. Dead men cannot catch fish.
Dead men have no need to fish. They are never hungry. *(Conchalla
starts laughing and climbs into steaming tub.)*
HENRY. Don't start that up again with me! There she goes! There
she goes again!
TAXI. Mr. Moss, I was wondering if maybe you could pay me for
the trip now and I could — *(Henry ignores Taxi. He takes fish over
to Conchalla in the tub and starts waving it in her face as Conchalla*

45

bathes.)

HENRY. She just refuses to recognize the simple truth of the thing. This is a genuine fish! A trophy fish! Look at the size of this fish!

CONCHALLA. I remember he bragged the same way about his penis.

HENRY. I never bragged about my penis! That's an outright lie! I never did that. *(To Taxi.)* She's lying again. Look at this fish!

CONCHALLA. That is a silly fish. That is a silly, silly fish. *(Conchalla suddenly snatches the fish out of Henry's grasp and flips it into the steaming water of the tub.)*

HENRY. *(To Taxi.)* Did you see that? Did you see what she did?

TAXI. Mr. Moss, I gotta get back to my girlfriend. I mean she's —

HENRY. She just threw my fish into the steaming water! My one and only fish!

CONCHALLA. There was no fish. You must have been dreaming!

HENRY. There was a fish! Everyone knows there was a fish! *(Henry makes a move toward Conchalla to retrieve his fish.)*

CONCHALLA. *(Fierce; her voice drops an octave.)* Don't you come near this fish! *(Henry freezes.)* I have it between my thighs now.

HENRY. Oh, she's disgusting.

CONCHALLA. Do you want it to come back to life?

HENRY. No! I don't want it to come back to life! I caught it! It's dead. I want it to stay dead.

CONCHALLA. I can bring it back to life for you. It is easy.

HENRY. I don't want it brought back to life! I'm gonna fry it up.

CONCHALLA. I just squeeze him a little between my legs. Like this —

HENRY. No!

TAXI. Mr. Moss, do you think we might be able to settle up here now? I need to get my money! I don't know how many times I gotta tell you.

HENRY. You'll get yer damn money! Not that you deserve it. What've you been doin' fer yer money? Huh? Sittin' around choking yer chicken! That's about it. Watching her continue to insult and berate me up one side of the river and down the other. Not once did you ever make so much as a gesture on my behalf! Not once!

TAXI. I'm a driver! I'm a taxicab driver! That's what I do. I drive people around from one place to another. That's all I do. I don't know about anything else. I don't know what you expect from me.

HENRY. I expect you to make a stand! That's what I expect. I've expected it all along! You told me you saw something in here. *(Points to his eyes.)* Something glimmering.

TAXI. I never said I saw something glimmering!

HENRY. That's what you said.

TAXI. I never said that!

HENRY. What'd you say, then?

TAXI. I said I saw nothing! Zero! Goose eggs. Absolutely nothing. It looked like a plain old everyday eyeball to me.

HENRY. I'm surrounded by liars! She says there's no fish, then there is a fish.

CONCHALLA. *(Laughs, looks down between her legs.)* It's starting to swim now.

HENRY. It can't be! It's dead. *(Henry moves toward Conchalla, but she stops him with a gesture.)*

CONCHALLA. *(Looking down at fish.)* Come take a look at your fish. It's peaceful now. It's happy. It has found its place in this world. Look at it swimming. Swimming, swimming. *(Pause.)*

TAXI. Mr. Moss, look — If you're not going to give me the money — I mean — just tell me what you want me to do. Just tell me and I'll do it. Okay? Then you can pay me and I'll get outta here. How's that sound? What exactly is it that you wanna convince her of?

HENRY. You ever been with a woman who thought you were dead?

TAXI. Well, no — I guess not. No.

HENRY. Then you don't know what it's like, do ya?

TAXI. No sir, but — I mean, there must've been a time when she thought you were alive. Right?

HENRY. I can't remember.

TAXI. Well — think back. Maybe if you could remember, then I could try to remind her.

HENRY. Remind her of what?

TAXI. Whatever it was. Was it your walk or something?

HENRY. My walk?

TAXI. Your talk?

HENRY. My talk?

TAXI. Well, I don't know — Was it your smile, maybe?

HENRY. *(Pushes Taxi away.)* Don't be an idiot!

TAXI. I'm just trying to help, is all!

HENRY. You're not trying to help! All you care about is your money! Your lousy money!

TAXI. I don't know exactly what it is you want me to do.

HENRY. Here's what I want you to do. Walk right over to her. Go ahead. Walk right over there to her, like a man, and explain the situation.

TAXI. What situation?

HENRY. What is the matter with you?

TAXI. You mean, explain to her that you're not dead?

HENRY. That's the ticket!

TAXI. How come you don't know that you're not dead? I don't get that.

HENRY. I know that I'm not dead! She's the one who doesn't know that I'm not dead! Now get on over there! Just take the plunge. *(Pause. Taxi very tentatively approaches Conchalla as she hums softly in the tub, oblivious to the others. Taxi stops. Taxi inches closer to Conchalla, who has her eyes closed, head resting back against the tub, very peacefully.)*

TAXI. Uh — Miss Lupina? *(No response from Conchalla. She just smiles, keeps her eyes closed and hums softly.)* Uh — ma'am — You don't really know me but — I'm — I'm the type a guy who calls a spade a spade. You know? I mean, I'm a pretty levelheaded, honest type a guy and —

HENRY. She doesn't give a shit what type a guy you are! You're supposed to be telling her about me! What about me?

TAXI. I was getting to that. I was just — Uh — Miss Lupina — There are certain signs of life that I think we can all agree on, aren't there? I mean, when you see someone breathing and — yelling and —

HENRY. Breathing and yelling? Breathing and yelling!

TAXI. *(To Henry.)* Yeah! Yeah, I mean, that's what you're doing! You're breathing and yelling so —

HENRY. That's not what I wanna be known for — Breathing and yelling! What the hell is that! I've got lots of qualities besides breathing and yelling! Tell her about those!

48

TAXI. I haven't seen those. *(Suddenly Conchalla lets out a gasp and raises her arm up out of the water with the fish dangling from her fingers. The fish is alive and twitching. She raises the fish directly over her head. Her eyes open, her mouth opens wide. Short pause, then she lets the fish drop directly into her mouth. Her jaws close as she grinds the fish between her teeth. Her arm drops with a mighty splash. Her eyes close again. She smiles as she goes on chewing the fish. Taxi runs toward the door, in terror. Henry storms toward Conchalla, but she remains undisturbed.)*
HENRY. *(To Conchalla.)* That was my fish she just ate!
TAXI. *(By door.)* All right! That's it! That's it — I'm leaving! This is not good for me! My girlfriend would not like me to be here with you people! She warned me about people like you. *(Suddenly the door swings open, almost knocking Taxi over. Esteban stands there in doorway with another bowl of steaming soup. Pause.)*
HENRY. *(To Esteban.)* What the hell're you doing here?
ESTEBAN. *(Smiling.)* Mr. Henry, I brought you some soup.
HENRY. I don't want any goddamn soup now! What're you doin', barging in here with soup? Can't you see we're busy! We're busy here!
ESTEBAN. *(Still in doorway.)* I saw the taxi and — I came over. I was worried for you.
CONCHALLA. *(From tub.)* Don't worry for the dead! Worry for the living!
ESTEBAN. Oh — She is here? Conchalla is here? *(Esteban gets very excited and steps into room, looking toward Conchalla.)*
HENRY. Yeah, she's here! She ate my fish! *(Conchalla cackles and splashes in the tub. Esteban heads toward her, slowly, carrying the soup in front of him.)*
ESTEBAN. I would have brought two bowls of soup. I did not know she was here.
CONCHALLA. Dead men can't eat soup!
HENRY. *(To Conchalla.)* Shut up with that!
TAXI. Mr. Moss, I'm asking you for the last time for my money. Ninety-six dollars and forty-two cents. That's what you owe me. *(Henry starts pulling out crumpled wet bills from his pockets and handing them over to Taxi as he speaks. Esteban keeps heading toward Conchalla, completely enraptured with her presence. Conchalla trickles water down her arms and sings to herself softly.)*

HENRY. All right, all right, all right! Stop whimpering about yer damn money.

ESTEBAN. If only I had known you were here. I would have made my *carne asada.*

HENRY. *(As he hands over money to Taxi.)* What did I ever do to deserve this? I've led an honorable life for the most part. I've served my country. I've dropped bombs on total strangers! I've worked my ass off for idiots. Paid my taxes. There's never once been any question of my — existence! Never once. It's humiliating! A man my age — to be forced into this kind of position. I'm too old to be having to prove I'm alive!

CONCHALLA. *(Laughing, sing-song.)* No one will come to his rescue! No one will come to his rescue.

ESTEBAN. The voice of an angel. *(Henry now seems to be talking to himself more than anyone else; staggering around, still doling out money to Taxi, who keeps counting it and asking for more. Esteban becomes more and more hypnotized by Conchalla.)*

HENRY. It's true — Maybe it's true — Maybe I am on the dark side of the moon now. It's possible. Maybe I am just — just completely — gone. *(Henry appeals to Esteban, but Esteban is locked onto Conchalla with his eyes. Taxi only wants the money. Suddenly Earl appears in the open doorway, extremely drunk. Henry freezes and stares at him. Ray immediately reacts to Earl's presence but still remains outside the action. He turns to face Earl, but Earl ignores him. Short pause as Earl just stands there, weaving slightly in doorway. Conchalla becomes alarmed at Earl's presence. She stands in the tub and yells at Esteban, who immediately reacts.)*

CONCHALLA. Get me my blanket! I need my blanket now! No one can even take a bath in peace. *(Esteban sets down the soup, rushes to bed and pulls the blanket off it, then takes it to Conchalla, who snatches it away from him and wraps herself up in it. She stays standing in tub. Henry staggers toward Earl.)*

HENRY. *(To Earl.)* What the hell're you doing, standing in my doorway? Who're you supposed to be?

EARL. I'm supposed to be your oldest son. That's who I'm supposed to be.

HENRY. *(Turning to Esteban.)* What is this? What's going on here?

ESTEBAN. I called him, Mr. Henry. I did not know what to do.

50

HENRY. *(Approaching Esteban.)* You called him?

ESTEBAN. I was worried something bad might have happened to you.

HENRY. Something bad? Something bad has just happened to me. Something bad is happening to me. Treachery from every angle! Sons! Neighbors! Women! Family! There's no end to it! How's a man supposed to breathe? *(Taxi exits and closes door behind him. Then the door closes, suddenly everyone freezes except Ray, who slowly crosses over to Earl and stops right in front of him, very close. He stares at Earl, then slowly reaches out and opens Earl's eyes very wide with his fingers and thumbs. This gesture should be reminiscent of Henry opening his eyes wide for Taxi to examine. Pause.)*

RAY. I see you, Earl. I see you now. *(Lights fade fast to black.)*

ACT THREE

Scene: Next morning. Same set. The photo album and tool chest are gone. Esteban is cooking menudo in a black pot on the stove. He has his spices, herbs and wears an orange apron. He is very meticulous and attentive to his cooking. Earl has a raging hangover. He lies on his back on Henry's bed, holding his head with both hands and writhing with pain. He moans and tries, with no effect, to kick his boots off. Esteban hums a sweet tune as he cooks. (Note: The cooking should be actual so that the smells of the menudo fill the room.)

EARL. *(Calling out to Esteban.)* The shoes! The shoes! Help me off with the damn shoes! *(Esteban reluctantly leaves his pot and goes to help Earl. He starts trying to pull Earl's boots off as Earl moans.)*
ESTEBAN. Oh, Mr. Earl, why you no come home when I tell you? Is no good to drink so much like that. You drink enough for ten men. We should have come home right after we make the phone call. Now we have miss everyone. Your father is gone. Your brother is gone.
EARL. *(Struggling to kick his boots off.)* They've always been gone! They were never here to begin with!
ESTEBAN. I feel bad we no here when your father they take him away. We should have been here for that, Mr. Earl. To see your father off.
EARL. *(Kicking out at Esteban.)* Get away from me! Just get the hell away! It's like being with a woman, being around you!
ESTEBAN. You cry for help — You chase me away. You chase me away — You cry for help. It's the same as your father.
EARL. *(Sitting up with a struggle.)* I am nothing like the old man! Get that into your fry-brain little mind! We're as different as chalk and cheese! I am nothing like the old man! *(Esteban backs off and returns to his cooking. Pause as Earl finishes kicking off one boot. He*

sits up on edge of bed, tries to steady his dizziness, clutches his head in agony.) Oh, my God! Feels like an ax in the back of my head. How'd you allow me to get into this kinda condition? Huh? You watch after Henry like a damn nanny goat, then you just turn my ass loose in every strange bar in creation. Where in the hell are your sense of values, man?

ESTEBAN. You wanted to go to those bars, Mr. Earl. You wanted to visit all of Henry's old bars. That's what you told me.

EARL. Now, why would I tell you something like that? Why would I give a shit about Henry's old bars?

ESTEBAN. You are asking me this?

EARL. I'm asking you. Yeah.

ESTEBAN. Menudo is almost ready.

EARL. I don't want any goddamn menudo! I'm asking you a question! Why would I wanna go around to Henry's old bars?

ESTEBAN. I have no idea, Mr. Earl. Maybe you thought you would — discover something.

EARL. Discover? Discover what?

ESTEBAN. Something about Henry.

EARL. *(Gives up pursuit.)* Ah, shit.

ESTEBAN. Menudo will cure you.

EARL. I told you, I don't want any a that goddamn stuff! What is that junk anyway? Boiled cow bellies? Where do you people come up with this shit? Who first thought of that? Boiled cow intestines! Jesus. It's primitive.

ESTEBAN. It will take away the pain.

EARL. I'm not eating any boiled cow guts! The brain of a man does not respond to the guts of a cow! Don't you know anything? *(Pause. Esteban keeps stirring the menudo. Earl nurses his head.)*

ESTEBAN. You are right about one thing.

EARL. What's that?

ESTEBAN. You are nothing like your father. You are worse than your father. At least with Henry you could have a conversation.

EARL. Oh yeah, he was a real conversationalist, wasn't he? Real gift for gab, old Henry. Just talk your head off on any damn subject. *(Pause.)* What was in it for you, anyway?

ESTEBAN. *Mande?*

EARL. What was in it for you? You and Henry. I mean all that sacrifice. Taking all that shit off a him all that time. What'd you ever have coming back?

ESTEBAN. *(Keeps stirring pot.)* I no understand, Mr. Earl.

EARL. What satisfaction could you possibly get outta serving a man who was so damn ungrateful!

ESTEBAN. It is like — feeding livestock — you know?

EARL. Feeding livestock?

ESTEBAN. Birds.

EARL. Birds?

ESTEBAN. They do nothing. They — live, that is all. They are just there. But they need you. They look to you. They wait for you by the fence. They know you bring them something. Every day they are there at the same time — waiting. They know the hour you will appear. Mr. Henry, he use to wait for me like that. I would see him standing by that window, looking toward my trailer. I would never tell him I see him waiting like that. He would be embarrassed; angry. But he look for me. I was the only one. He have no one else. Then — sometimes late at night, I come over and we sit. We just sit here at that table, facing the moon. We listen to the radio. We no speak. Sometimes we no speak for hours. Just listen. Music from deep in Mexico.

EARL. But every now and then you'd have a conversation right? You were saying you used to have conversations —

ESTEBAN. Sometimes. Sometimes Henry he ask me about my pueblo — Where I come from. My people, my family. He never talk about himself. He say he have no past. Mostly we just listen. Dogs. Coyotes. *La musica.* It was peaceful.

EARL. Peaceful? Henry?

ESTEBAN. The two of us.

EARL. Peaceful. That'd be something, wouldn't it?

ESTEBAN. What?

EARL. Peace. *(Pause.)*

ESTEBAN. Ay. Menudo. *(Returns to stove. Esteban keeps stirring pot. Earl gazes around room, then suddenly notices the missing toolbox and photo album. He stands fast and moves shakily toward table.)*

EARL. That son of a bitch took everything! Look! He took the tools and the album. And the bottle! He took the damn bottle too! Those didn't belong to him! Nobody said he could have that stuff!

54

Who in the hell does he think he is? He's absconded with every-thing! Look at this!

ESTEBAN. Maybe he was only cleaning up.

EARL. Cleaning up? He's ripped me off! He doesn't deserve any of that stuff! That was mine! That belonged to me! I inherited it fair and square! I was the one who stuck it out here with Henry. Not him!

ESTEBAN. I am very sorry we miss him. I wanted to say good-bye.

EARL. Who?

ESTEBAN. Mr. Henry.

EARL. He was dead! You don't say good-bye to a dead man! It's too late. I'm talking about my brother now. My living, breathing conniving brother!

ESTEBAN. In my village we always say good-bye to the dead.

EARL. This is not your village. We're across the river here.

ESTEBAN. They will come back to haunt you if you do not say good-bye.

EARL. Will you knock it off with that! Dead is dead, all right? Finished. *Terminado.*

ESTEBAN. Maybe.

EARL. Maybe nothing.

ESTEBAN. Maybe Henry was waiting to say good-bye and we weren't here.

EARL. Jesus H. Christ! Just — Just — stir your damn pot, will you! Just — *(Earl sits down heavily in upstage chair and holds his throbbing head between his hands. Long pause as Esteban continues to stir his pot.)*

ESTEBAN. *(Stirring.)* We had a cousin, Manolito, once, who died from a green snake. No one said good-bye to him. There was superstition about the snake and no one said good-bye. The next day a hawk appeared above the door of his uncle's house. Every day the hawk would shit on his uncle's head just as he stepped out-side. Every single day. That went on for over a month. This is the kind of thing that can happen when you don't say good-bye to the dead. You get shit on by a hawk. *(Short pause. Earl lowers his hands and looks at Esteban. Suddenly Ray enters with a bag of groceries and closes door behind him. He stops and stares at Earl. Earl stays seated.)*

Esteban turns and stares at Ray.)
RAY. How's it going? *(Ray crosses to refrigerator, opens it and starts unloading groceries into it. Pause.)*
EARL. "How's it going?" That's all you've got to say? "How's it going?"
RAY. *(Unloading groceries.)* Well, I was thinking about "How ya doing?" or "What's goin' on?" or "Where you been so long?"
EARL. What're you doing back here?
RAY. Stockin' up the larder. Puttin' in a few supplies. I made kind of a big decision last night. It just came on me.
EARL. Yeah, what decision's that?
RAY. I'm gonna stay awhile. *(Pause. Earl stares at Ray, who keeps unloading groceries and putting them in fridge. Esteban keeps stirring.)*
EARL. You're gonna stay?
RAY. Yep.
EARL. You mean here? You're gonna stay here in this house? Henry's house?
RAY. Yep. I like it here.
EARL. Oh, so now you like it here. It's warm and cozy.
RAY. I dunno. I feel — some kind of connection here.
EARL. Connection?
RAY. Yep.
EARL. I suppose you felt some kind of "connection" to the tools and the photo album too, huh? And the bottle. My bottle.
RAY. Oh — Yeah, well — I gave those away.
EARL. *(Moving toward Ray.)* What?
RAY. I gave 'em away to that taxicab driver.
EARL. What taxicab driver!
RAY. You know, the guy who uh — took Dad fishing. *(Pause.)*
EARL. What're you talking about?
RAY. The guy — the driver who came and picked Dad up. You know. *(Pause.)*
EARL. You — found him?
RAY. Yep.
EARL. What do you mean? How'd you find him?
RAY. Tracked him down. Like I said. Through the company. Made some phone calls down there at the Sonic. I looked all over the place for you guys but I guess you were, uh "celebrating" or

56

something, huh?

EARL. You found the taxicab driver who took Henry fishing?

RAY. That's what I said, yeah. Amazing huh?

EARL. You actually went all the way out of your way to find the taxicab driver who took Henry fishing? *(Ray finishes with groceries, closes refrigerator, takes a Coke with him, crosses to Earl, stops in front of Earl and raps on Earl's forehead like he was knocking on a door.)*

RAY. What is it, Earl — liquor or genetics that makes you so thick? *(Ray crosses to table, sits and opens Coke, takes a drink.)*

EARL. So — So what'd he do? You talk to him?

RAY. Yeah. Sure I talked to him. What is that stink?

ESTEBAN. Menudo.

RAY. Really stinks.

EARL. *(Moving toward Ray.)* So, what'd he say — this taxicab driver? He tell you anything different than what I told you?

RAY. Now why would he do that?

EARL. I don't know why he'd do that! Just to — confuse the issue probably. People are always making up stuff.

RAY. What issue?

EARL. You know — the issue — the whole situation. The perdicament here!

RAY. I didn't know there was a perdicament here, Earl.

EARL. There isn't a perdicament here but he could've made it seem like there was a perdicament here! He could've twisted things around!

RAY. He just told me what happened, that's all. Simple story.

EARL. *(Pause.)* So — Everything matched up, right? I mean everything he told you was the same thing I told you, right?

RAY. Pretty much. *(Pause.)*

EARL. What the hell are you doing giving away our father's belongings to a complete stranger? That's what I wanna know. What kind of a stunt is that?

RAY. I didn't think they meant anything to you.

EARL. There were photographs in there going back to the turn of the century!

RAY. Yeah. That's a long time ago.

EARL. You're goddamn right that's a long time ago! Those photographs are irreplaceable. Now some total stranger's got ahold of them. An outsider!

RAY. Well, he can always make up some kind of a story about them.

EARL. What's that supposed to mean?

RAY. He can tell people they're pictures of his family. His ancestors. He can make up a whole tall tale.

EARL. Why would he wanna do that?

RAY. Maybe he's got no family. Maybe he needs to make one up.

EARL. If he's got no family he can't make one up! That's not something you make up outta thin air! You can't make that stuff up. It's too complicated!

RAY. People will believe anything, Earl. You know that. Look at all the stuff you've told me.

EARL. What stuff?

RAY. Over the years. All the bullshit you've told me. I believed every word.

EARL. You know what? You're beginning to make me a little bit sick to my stomach. Ever since you arrived here — You come in here with this — this — "atmosphere" around you. This suspicion. Right off the bat. Everybody's under suspicion. You don't have one clue about what's gone on here — about what me and Esteban have been through. You just waltz in here and start judging — Passing judgment!

RAY. I've got a clue, Earl. I've got a big clue. *(Pause. The brothers stare at each other. Esteban very quietly stirs his pot, trying to become invisible. Pause. Earl shakes his head in disgust.)*

ESTEBAN. Menudo is almost ready!

EARL. *(Turning on Esteban.)* I don't want any menudo! I told you that! I'm not interested in menudo! If you mention menudo one more time I'm gonna rip your guts out and throw them in that pot! *(Earl clutches his head in pain. He returns to Henry's bed and crashes. Writhing on bed.)* Oh, my God. Oh, my God, my God, my God!

RAY. *(At table, sipping Coke.)* Too much party, Earl? You're a little old to be hitting the sauce like that. What were you uh "celebrating" exactly? The removal of the corpse?

EARL. *(On bed.)* You get outta here now! Go someplace else! There's lots of motels in this town. You just get outta here!

RAY. Or were you uh — thinking maybe you got away with something? (*Pause. Earl struggles to sit up on the bed. He finally makes it and sits there, facing Ray.*)

EARL. What'd this joker tell you? This taxicab driver? He told you something, didn't he?

RAY. Now, what would he tell me, Earl?

EARL. (*Standing, shaky.*) He put some idea in your head!

RAY. I got my own ideas, Earl. I don't need any new ones.

EARL. He was an idiot, that guy! A total idiot!

RAY. Oh, so you met him then? You were here the same time he was, huh?

EARL. I didn't — I didn't meet him! Henry told me about him.

RAY. Henry?

EARL. I mean — Esteban! Esteban told me he was an idiot! (*To Esteban.*) Didn't you? (*No answer from Esteban.*) Didn't you tell me that! You told me the guy was a total jerk.

RAY. Well, which was it — a jerk or an idiot?

EARL. (*To Ray.*) You're trying to turn this thing into something that it wasn't!

RAY. What was it, Earl? What exactly was it? (*Earl charges Ray but Ray dodges him quickly and is out of the chair in a flash.*)

EARL. I want you outta here! I want you the hell outta here now! (*Earl crashes into the table and crumples on top of it, exhausted. Ray slowly circles him. Pause. Esteban turns the fire off under his pot. Ray keeps circling Earl, who remains sprawled out on top of the table.*)

ESTEBAN. I will come back later.

RAY. (*Keeps circling.*) No, you just keep cooking, Esteban. No reason to stop cooking.

ESTEBAN. I think I should go back to my trailer, Mr. Ray.

EARL. (*Collapsed on table.*) My legs. I can't feel my legs!

RAY. Get off the table, Earl. What do you think this is, a flophouse or something? A drunk tank!

EARL. Something's happened to my legs!

RAY. Get off the table! (*Ray kicks Earl's feet out from under him. Earl crashes to the floor. Esteban moves toward door. Pause.*)

ESTEBAN. I have no reason to be here, Mr. Ray.

RAY. None of us do, Esteban. That's the truth of it, isn't it? We're all just hanging around now. The old man's dead. (*Esteban crosses back to stove, turns it on and continues stirring pot. Earl stays on floor.*)

EARL. *(On floor.)* Something's really gone wrong with my legs, Ray. I'm not kidding you. I don't know what it is.

RAY. Get up off the floor, Earl. You're a full-grown man.

EARL. *(Stays on floor.)* I — I think we should call somebody.

RAY. Get up off the floor! *(Ray kicks Earl hard in the ribs. Earl struggles to the downstage chair and drags himself up into it. Esteban keeps stirring.)* You know what I think? I think it's time we straightened up in here, don't you? Get a little order. I mean if I'm gonna be living here I'd like to have a little order. Scrub the floors maybe. The windows. Brighten the place up a bit. What do you think? How 'bout it, Esteban? You got a bucket around? A mop? *(Pause. Esteban and Earl stare at him like he's lost his mind.)* No mop?

ESTEBAN. No mop, Mr. Ray.

RAY. No mop. How 'bout some rags, then? Must be some old rags around. Well, this will work. *(Ray rips the apron off Esteban and balls it up. He crosses to Earl, crushing the apron between his hands.)* Now, here's what we're gonna do, Earl. This is my house now. So I want it clean. It's only natural. I want it spotless. I want it so you can eat right off the floor. So you can see the sun bounce off every little nook and cranny. Now, I want you to take this apron and get it wet. *(Ray grabs Earl by the hair, shoves the apron into Earl's face and drags Earl over to the tub. He turns the hot water on and forces Earl to soak the apron in it.)*

ESTEBAN. *(At stove, crossing himself frantically.)* Jesus, Maria, Jose! Jesus, Maria, Jose! Jesus, Maria, Jose!

RAY. *(At tub, forcing Earl.)* Get it wet now, Earl. Get it nice and wet and wring it out. Scrub every inch of this floor till it shines like new money! That's what I want you to do, Earl. I want you to do that for me, right now. *(Pause. Earl follows Ray's orders. Ray smiles at Esteban and crosses to him. Ray smells the pot of menudo and pats Esteban on the back.)* Stuff really stinks bad, Esteban. Is it supposed to smell like that? Smells like something dead. *(Earl begins slowly scrubbing floor with wet apron, on his hands and knees. Ray moves to tub and shuts the water off.)* This whole house stinks. Why is that? Is that from all your cooking, Esteban — over the years? Years and years of soups and chili and beans and shit? All that cooking. For what? What'd you think you were gonna do? Save Henry's puny life? Is that what you thought?

EARL. I'm really serious about my legs, Ray. They've gone numb. *(Ray suddenly kicks the bed. Earl stops scrubbing but stays on his hands and knees. Esteban is backed up to the stove.)*
RAY. Just keep scrubbing, Earl. We may have to disinfect this whole house. We may have to tear the walls down and rebuild the whole son of a bitch. Just to get the stink outta here. What is that stink? Can't you smell that? What smells like that? Maybe it's you, Earl. Is it you that smells like that? *(Earl starts scrubbing the floor again. Ray goes to him, bends down and smells Earl all over as Earl continues scrubbing.)* Esteban — Come over here and smell Earl. See what you think. Come on over here. *(Esteban reluctantly crosses to Earl and Ray. To Esteban.)* Now, just bend down here and smell him. I can't tell anymore. I've lost track. What's he smell like to you? *(Esteban bends over and smells Earl, who continues scrubbing floor. Esteban straightens up and stares at Ray.)* Well?
ESTEBAN. Just — like a man, Mr. Ray.
RAY. A man! Is that what a man smells like? *(Ray bends over and takes a long whiff of Earl, who keeps right on scrubbing through all this. Ray straightens up.)* Nah, I dunno — Smells rotten to me. *(Earl stops scrubbing.)*
EARL. Look — I'm not feeling so good. That tequila messed me up. I'm not used to that stuff. *(Ray kicks Earl in the ass.)*
RAY. Keep scrubbing, Earl! Just keep yer nose to the grindstone. There's a lotta territory to cover here. Lots of square footage. *(Earl starts scrubbing floor again. Esteban returns to his place by the stove. Ray moves around the room.)* You remember how Mom used to work at it, don't ya?
EARL. *(Scrubbing.)* Mom?
RAY. Yeah. You remember how she used to scrub, day in and day out. Scrub, scrub, scrub.
EARL. I don't remember.
RAY. You remember. You remember how she used to get everything spit-shined and polished — everything gleaming. The floors. The curtains. The tablecloth starched. All the glasses shining. *(Throughout this sequence the tempo of Earl's scrubbing increases with the force of Ray's pursuit. Ray moves freely around the space.)*
EARL. No —
RAY. You remember. Potatoes steaming on the plates. Carrots.

61

Everything waiting. Everything perfect and just waiting like some kind of picture. You remember all that.

EARL. No —

RAY. And then — I used to think — I used to think she was doing all that for us, you know. You and me. I used to think she was going through all this work — all this preparation for us. And then, one day, it just — hit me. I don't know why. I just suddenly saw that it wasn't for us at all. It was for him. It was for Henry. Everything. All those hours and hours, slaving away — Slaving away. It was for him.

EARL. I don't remember that.

RAY. And then — And then, here he'd come! Bustin' in the door. You remember. *(Ray rushes to the door, opens and slams it, then turns himself into drunken Henry, staggering into the room. Earl keeps scrubbing. Impersonating Henry:)* "What the hell is everyone waitin' on me for? What're you waitin' on? The food's hot! Sit down and eat the food. Jesus H. Christ! You'd think this was some kinda goddamn formal dinner here or something. You're hungry aren't ya? Sit down and eat!" *(Drops impersonation.)* And then everybody'd scramble to the table while he'd stomp the shit off his boots and throw his coat on the floor. You remember that? You remember how we'd all just sit there staring down into our napkins while he went on ranting and raving about the lack of rain or the price of citrus or the cost of feeding useless sons! Do you remember that, Earl! Do you remember that at all!

EARL. *(Still scrubbing.)* No, I don't remember! I don't remember any of that. You must've been alone. I must've been out someplace.

RAY. You were there, Earl. You were there the whole time. I remember your breath. The sound of your breath. Chopping away. I remember thinking, "He must be just as scared as me to be breathing like that. Just as full of terror!" But then I thought, "No, that's not possible. He's bigger than me. He's my big brother. How could he be scared?" And when she started screaming I thought Earl's gonna stand up for her. Earl's gonna take the weight. Earl's gonna stop him somehow!

EARL. I wasn't there for that! I was never there!

RAY. Because I knew, see — I knew I didn't have a chance against him. I barely came up to his waist. All I could do is watch! And there she was — On the floor! Just like you, Earl. Just like you are now. Backed up under the sink! Crushed. He was kicking her, Earl! He was kicking her just like this! *(Ray starts savagely kicking Earl all over the stage. Earl scrambles on his hands and knees but Ray is relentless. Esteban cowers and stays clear.)* And every time he kicked her his rage grew a little bit and his face changed! His eyes bulged out and the blood rushed into his neck! And her blood was flying all over the kitchen, Earl!

EARL. *(Scrambling away on hands and knees.)* That wasn't me that was doing that! That wasn't me! That was him! *(Ray suddenly stops kicking Earl. They are both panting for breath.)*

RAY. And still I kept thinking — I kept thinking — sooner or later Earl's gonna step in. Earl's gonna stop him. Earl's not going to let this happen. And just then — I looked out the kitchen window and I saw your car — your little white Chevy. Kicking up dust the whole length of the hay field. And that's the last time I saw you, Earl. That's the last time I saw you for a long, long while.

EARL. *(Still on floor.)* I never ran! I never ran! *(Short pause, then Henry suddenly blasts through the door with Conchalla close behind, still wrapped up in the blanket. Ray moves immediately extreme downstage and becomes witness again. He faces audience the whole time. Earl remains on the floor. Lights shift. Soft spot on Ray. Esteban hangs near the stove. Conchalla goes to the bed and flops down on it. Henry approaches Earl. Both Henry and Conchalla are as drunk as the last time we saw them. Henry stops in front of Earl and sniffs the air.)*

HENRY. What stinks? What's that stink in here?

ESTEBAN. Menudo, Mr. Henry.

HENRY. Well turn that shit off! Smells like a goddamn Tijuana whorehouse in here. Turn it off! *(Esteban turns off the stove.)*

ESTEBAN. I was making it for Mr. Earl.

HENRY. What's a matter with "Mr. Earl"? What's he doing crawling around on my floor? *(To Earl.)* What're you doing down there?

EARL. I've lost track.

HENRY. Well get the hell up off my floor! This isn't some kind of a New York City crash pad or something. Have some respect. I've got a woman in the house, in case you didn't notice.

CONCHALLA. *(Calling out from bed.)* A woman! A woman in the house! *(Earl drags himself up from floor and just stands there.)*

HENRY. *(To Earl.)* What's the deal here anyway? You showing up outta the blue like this. What's the big idea?

EARL. Esteban told me it was an emergency.

HENRY. Emergency! He's a Mexican! Everything's an emergency with them.

EARL. He said you'd disappeared.

HENRY. Since when did you ever give two shits whether I disappeared or not? I haven't seen hide nor hair of you for how long's it been now?

EARL. I forget.

HENRY. Yeah. Me too.

EARL. I wasn't — sure you wanted to see me.

HENRY. Oh, is that right? You weren't sure. Well, let's get clear about this then. Let's get this straight once and for all. Far as I'm concerned you never even existed! You were one big bad mistake! All right? Does that make any kind of sense to you at all?

EARL. Yeah. Yeah, that makes sense. That explains a whole lot.

HENRY. Good. Now you can clear on outta here because everything's just hunky-dory. Why in the hell does that stuff stink so bad? *(Henry crosses to Esteban. Conchalla giggles and turns over on the bed. To Esteban.)* What're you doin' here anyway? Why are you always here, stickin' yer nose into my business? Don't you have your own place? What is it about my place that's so damn attractive?

CONCHALLA. There is a woman! A woman in the house!

HENRY. *(To Conchalla.)* You pipe down! *(Conchalla rises from the bed and offers her arm out to Esteban.)*

CONCHALLA. I will take you to your trailer, Esteban. Come on. *(Esteban starts to cross to door but Conchalla intercepts him and throws her arms around him. Holding Esteban.)* I will take you there and bounce you on my knees! *(She squeezes Esteban in a bear hug and bounces him up and down. As she bounces Esteban:)* Wouldn't you like some bouncing? I will bounce you all night long until the sun explodes! Wouldn't you like that? Wouldn't you like some of that, Esteban?

HENRY. Knock it off! Knock it off! *(Conchalla stops bouncing Esteban and throws him backward onto the bed.)* He doesn't need any bouncing! *(Conchalla slowly approaches Esteban on bed.)*

CONCHALLA. He looks to me like a man who could use some

bouncing. Look how flat he is.

HENRY. If there's any bouncing going on here I'll be the one in charge of it. *(Conchalla turns to Henry.)*

CONCHALLA. *(To Henry.)* Oh, you'll be the one?

HENRY. That's right. *(Now Conchalla approaches Henry, slow and seductive. Esteban gets up from bed and heads for the door.)*

CONCHALLA. *(Approaching Henry.)* You'll be the one in charge of bouncing? The Captain of Bouncing! I didn't know dead men were any good at bouncing. I thought their bouncing days were over.

HENRY. *(Appealing to Earl.)* There she goes again! She won't give it up. She goes around and around and around about it. She ate my fish, you know.

EARL. What?

HENRY. My fish I caught. She ate it. Raw! She's a barbarian! *(Henry crosses to bed and collapses on it. Pause as Earl just stands there, not knowing what to do with his father.)*

EARL. You need anything, Dad?

HENRY. *(Stays on bed.)* What!

EARL. You need something? You want me to get you something?

HENRY. Yeah — Most likely I do. Most likely I need something. I've got that feeling. What would it be? What would it be that I need? *(Pause. Earl moves closer to Henry, who remains crumpled on the bed. Earl stops.)*

EARL. You need a blanket or something?

HENRY. She's got the blanket! She takes everything. The blanket. The bottle. My fish.

EARL. Who is she, anyway?

HENRY. Who is she?

EARL. Yeah. I mean — I had no idea you were living with a woman.

HENRY. I'm not living with her! Don't be ridiculous. How could you live with something like that?

EARL. Well, whatever you call it.

HENRY. You don't call it living! *(Henry rolls over and sits up unsteadily. He stares at Earl.)* I don't suppose you've got a bottle, do ya?

EARL. No, I —

HENRY. Nah, you wouldn't have a bottle. You don't have a pot to piss in. *(Henry gets up and staggers toward refrigerator. He opens*

it and stares into it. Earl watches him. Staring into fridge.) What're
you doin' out here, anyway? Why'd you come all the way out here?
EARL. Esteban — He called me. He said you were in trouble or
something. He said you'd disappeared. *(Henry laughs and slams
refrigerator shut. Turns to Earl.)*
HENRY. Disappeared! Disappeared?
EARL. Yeah. That's what he said.
HENRY. *(Staggers toward Earl.)* Have you ever known anybody
who's disappeared? Huh? *(He stops.)* Just — vanished?
EARL. No —
HENRY. No. That's not possible is it? Is that a possible thing for
a human being? Just — disappear?
EARL. I don't know. I mean, I guess there have been —
HENRY. What?
EARL. Cases.
HENRY. Disappearing cases?
EARL. Yeah. *(Henry staggers closer to Earl and stops.)*
HENRY. Are you — Are you seeing me, right now?
EARL. What?
HENRY. Are you seeing me; perceiving me as we speak?
EARL. Well, yeah — Sure.
HENRY. You're sure?
EARL. Yeah. Why?
HENRY. You're convinced that I'm standing here before you?
That I'm an actuality in this world?
EARL. Yeah.
HENRY. What's giving you that impression?
EARL. What?
HENRY. That I'm here. That I'm real? What's convincing you of
that?
EARL. I — I recognize you.
HENRY. You do?
EARL. Yeah.
HENRY. What do you recognize? What is it?
EARL. I remember —
HENRY. What?
EARL. Your voice. Your eyes. The — smell.
HENRY. The smell? What smell?

EARL. That — that —
HENRY. Booze?
EARL. No.
HENRY. What, then?
EARL. Some — some — scent of you.
HENRY. A scent? You mean like a dog or something?
EARL. No — *(Suddenly Henry throws his arms around Earl and squeezes him in a bear hug. Earl panics but can't get out of it.)*
HENRY. *(Squeezing Earl.)* You mean like a dog, don't ya? Like a mad dog?
EARL. *(Struggling.)* No! Let go a me for God's sake!
HENRY. *(Still squeezing Earl in his grip.)* Like a dead man! Is that what you think? You ever known a dead man with a grip like this? *(Earl finally breaks free and shoves Henry back. They stand apart.)* You shouldn't take it personal.
EARL. That woman —
HENRY. Yeah. She's somethin', huh? Conchalla Lupina. Ever seen anything like her?
EARL. No — No, I never did.
HENRY. She'd scare the pants off a natural man. You probably couldn't handle a woman like that.
EARL. No, probably not. Where'd you meet her, anyway?
HENRY. Where'd I meet her? Where do ya suppose I'd meet her?
EARL. I have no idea. *(Henry begins to slowly approach Earl. At the same time, the door swings open and Conchalla is standing there watching. Henry's back is to her, but Earl can see her in the doorway. She takes sips from a bottle of tequila.)*
HENRY. *(As he moves to Earl.)* I was — "obliterated," as they say. Absolutely sloshed. Been in and outta that drunk tank down there for over a month. This time though — I woke up — she was on top a me. *(Laughs.)* She had me straddled!
EARL. *(Trying to end the story.)* All right, all right!
CONCHALLA. *(Giggles in doorway.)* He couldn't resist me! I was too much woman! *(Henry doesn't look back to Conchalla but keeps his focus on Earl. Earl backs away.)*
HENRY. I couldn't resist. It's true. There she was — big as day!
EARL. I — I don't really wanna hear about it, okay? *(Conchalla enters room and closes door behind her. She keeps sipping from bottle*

and smiling at Earl.)

HENRY. Big as the damn Sangre de Cristo mountains! Right on top a me. What could I do?

CONCHALLA. He was whimpering when they threw him in. Hunched up in a corner, whining like a puppy.

HENRY. I wasn't whimpering. I had the shakes. Cold.

CONCHALLA. He was whimpering.

HENRY. *(Approaching Earl.)* Huddled up — trying to get some warmth. Just trying to find some warmth — that's all.

CONCHALLA. I gave him warmth.

EARL. *(Trying to escape them.)* That's enough!

CONCHALLA. I gave him so much warmth, he passed out. He couldn't take my warmth! *(Conchalla giggles as she and Henry close in on Earl.)*

HENRY. I could take it. I could take it.

CONCHALLA. When I dismounted him, his heart stopped. His breath. Nothing was moving.

EARL. I don't wanna hear anymore of this! I don't wanna hear anymore! All right? Stop telling me about this! Just stop telling me about all this! *(Henry and Conchalla stop suddenly. Henry notices Conchalla's bottle and approaches her, trying to get a hit off it, but she hides it behind her back. After pause.)* Look — for some strange reason or other, I still remember my mother, okay?

HENRY. Your mother?

EARL. Yeah. Yeah, that's right. My mother. I can still — picture her. I can — see her. I can —

HENRY. Your mother.

EARL. She was always —

HENRY. What?

EARL. Faithful. She was always faithful. No matter what. I remember her now. I remember her on her hands and knees.

HENRY. Your mother. That little shit. *(Conchalla giggles, drinks, goes to bed and flops down on it.)* Another traitor. Locked me out of my own house! That's what she did. Locked me out!

EARL. I remember that too.

HENRY. You remember nothin'! Your "mother." Wasn't for her, I wouldn't be in this mess I'm in right now. This whole situation!

EARL. How is she to blame for that?

68

HENRY. She caused me to leave! She caused me to pack on outta there! What'd'ya think? You think I wanted to wander around this Christless country for twenty-some years like a refugee? Like some miserable fuckin' exile? Huh? You think I wanted that? She did that to me! She banished me! She turned me out!

EARL. You broke the place up. You smashed all the windows!

HENRY. SHE LOCKED ME OUT! *(Henry collapses, grabs onto the upstage chair and crashes to his knees. Earl moves toward him, but Conchalla stops him.)*

CONCHALLA. Don't touch him!

HENRY. *(On his knees, clutching chair.)* She locked me out that's what she did to me. Locked me out completely.

CONCHALLA. Now he will start to crumble — to whimper. The same. Always the same.

EARL. Dad? You want a doctor or something? You wanna go to the hospital? *(Conchalla laughs and drinks from bottle.)*

CONCHALLA. The hospital! He is way beyond the hospital! *(Conchalla grabs Henry by the chest with tremendous force and lifts him up to the table. She lays him out on his back on the table as Earl watches helplessly.)*

EARL. What the hell're you doing to him! Haven't you done enough damage already? *(Conchalla giggles and strokes Henry's hair gently. Then she lifts his head and starts pouring the tequila into his mouth very gently, like medicine. Henry gurgles.)*

CONCHALLA. Damage? I have done no damage. I am just watching out for the dead. Do you know how much trouble that is? Watching — always watching? It takes a lot of time. A lot of patience.

EARL. Stop it! Stop giving him that! *(Earl lunges toward Conchalla, trying to grab the bottle away from her, but she lets out a bloodcurdling scream and freezes Earl in his tracks. She giggles. She strokes Henry's face very gently.)*

CONCHALLA. I will show you your father. You see him now? You see how he looks to me. Helpless. Hoping. Dreaming. Wishing for death. Wishing for some way out. *(Stroking Henry's head.)* It takes courage, no? I gave him courage. A drowned man. He comes up for air. He gasps — *(Conchalla keeps pouring tequila down Henry as she straddles him. Stroking Henry's head.)* Now he begins to go back home. Now — he begins to return. You will see.

69

He remembers now.

HENRY. *(Spitting to get his throat clear.)* I remember — The day I died — She was on the floor.

CONCHALLA. *(Gently.)* Now, he sees. *(Henry sits up on table with Conchalla supporting him and gently stroking his head as Earl watches.)*

HENRY. I remember the floor — was yellow — I can see the floor and — her blood — her blood was smeared across it. I thought I'd killed her — but it was me. It was me I killed. *(Conchalla kisses Henry lightly on the forehead and lifts him off the table. Henry stands there, looking out.)* I can see her eyes — peering up at me. Her swollen eyes. She just — stays there, under the sink. Silent. Balled up like an animal. Nothing moving but her eyes. She sees me. She knows. I can tell she knows. She sees me dying! Right there in front of her. She watches me pass away! There's nothing she can do. And then — there's this flash of grief — from her. Grief! Why would she grieve for me? *(Earl heads for the door.)*

EARL. I can't listen to this anymore! *(Conchalla moves fast in front of Earl and stops him.)*

CONCHALLA. *(To Earl.)* You watch.

HENRY. I ran out into the yard and I remember — I remember this — death. I remember it now — Cut off. Everything — far away. Birds. Trees. Sky. Removed! Everything — out beyond reach. And I ran. I ran to the car and I drove. I drove for days with the windows wide open. The wind beating across my eyes — my face. I had no map. No destination. I just drove. *(Conchalla begins humming a death song and sways from side to side. She moves to Henry and hands him the bottle. Henry takes it and drinks. To Earl.)* You could've stopped me then but you didn't.

EARL. What? What're you talking about? *(Henry turns with bottle and moves toward Earl but trying more to get to the bed. Earl backs away from him. Conchalla continues to sway and hum her song.)*

HENRY. *(To Earl.)* You were there. You were there watching the whole time. I remember your beady eyes peering out at me from the hallway. You saw the whole thing.

EARL. I don't know what you're talking about!

HENRY. You saw! I looked straight at you! You looked straight back. Your mother was screaming the whole time!

EARL. No! I was never there. I was never there for that!

70

HENRY. You coulda stopped me but you didn't. *(Henry almost loses his balance and crashes, but he staggers to the bed and goes down on top of it.)*
EARL. I couldn't. I — I — I was scared. I was — just — too — scared.
HENRY. You were scared! A what? A me? You were scared of a dead man? *(Henry takes a last giant pull on the bottle, then lies back and dies quietly. Conchalla stops humming her song. She moves to Henry and covers him with the blanket. She turns to Earl.)*
CONCHALLA. *(To Earl.)* The body — it stays. For three whole days no one must touch him. Not you. No one. You are the keeper. You watch now. *(Conchalla exits. Pause. Earl moves to bed and sits down next to Henry's corpse, facing directly out to audience. Pause. Ray turns to Earl but stays in his spot of light. Earl stares straight out.)*
RAY. Well, you know me, Earl — I was never one to live in the past. That was never my deal. You know — You remember how I was.
EARL. Yeah. Yeah, right. I remember. *(Lights fade slowly to black.)*

End of Play

PROPERTY LIST

Bottle of alcohol
Blanket (HENRY, ESTEBAN)
Photo album (EARL, TAXI)
Tool chest and tools (RAY, TAXI)
Jar of jalapeño peppers (RAY)
Bowl of soup (ESTEBAN)
Soup spoon (ESTEBAN)
Napkin (ESTEBAN)
Salt shaker (ESTEBAN)
Black canvas body bag (ATTENDANTS)
Stretcher (ATTENDANTS)
Money (HENRY, TAXI)
Small fish (HENRY)
Washcloth (CONCHALLA)
Pot (ESTEBAN)
Knife (ESTEBAN)
Vegetables (ESTEBAN)
Cutting board (ESTEBAN)
Spoon (ESTEBAN)
Bag of groceries (RAY)
Coke (RAY)
Kitchen towel (ESTEBAN)

SOUND EFFECTS

Drum roll
Mexican rhumba music
Mariachi music

NEW PLAYS

★ **MOTHERHOOD OUT LOUD by Leslie Ayvazian, Brooke Berman, David Cale, Jessica Goldberg, Beth Henley, Lameece Issaq, Claire LaZebnik, Lisa Loomer, Michele Lowe, Marco Pennette, Theresa Rebeck, Luanne Rice, Annie Weisman and Cheryl L. West, conceived by Susan R. Rose and Joan Stein.** When entrusting the subject of motherhood to such a dazzling collection of celebrated American writers, what results is a joyous, moving, hilarious, and altogether thrilling theatrical event. "Never fails to strike both the funny bone and the heart." *—BackStage.* "Packed with wisdom, laughter, and plenty of wry surprises." *—TheaterMania.* [1M, 3W] ISBN: 978-0-8222-2589-8

★ **COCK by Mike Bartlett.** When John takes a break from his boyfriend, he accidentally meets the girl of his dreams. Filled with guilt and indecision, he decides there is only one way to straighten this out. "[A] brilliant and blackly hilarious feat of provocation." *—Independent.* "A smart, prickly and rewarding view of sexual and emotional confusion." *—Evening Standard.* [3M, 1W] ISBN: 978-0-8222-2766-3

★ **F. Scott Fitzgerald's THE GREAT GATSBY adapted for the stage by Simon Levy.** Jay Gatsby, a self-made millionaire, passionately pursues the elusive Daisy Buchanan. Nick Carraway, a young newcomer to Long Island, is drawn into their world of obsession, greed and danger. "Levy's combination of narration, dialogue and action delivers most of what is best in the novel." *—Seattle Post-Intelligencer.* "A beautifully crafted interpretation of the 1925 novel which defined the Jazz Age." *—London Free Press.* [5M, 4W] ISBN: 978-0-8222-2727-4

★ **LONELY, I'M NOT by Paul Weitz.** At an age when most people are discovering what they want to do with their lives, Porter has been married and divorced, earned seven figures as a corporate "ninja," and had a nervous breakdown. It's been four years since he's had a job or a date, and he's decided to give life another shot. "Critic's pick!" *—NY Times.* "An enjoyable ride." *—NY Daily News.* [3M, 3W] ISBN: 978-0-8222-2734-2

★ **ASUNCION by Jesse Eisenberg.** Edgar and Vinny are not racist. In fact, Edgar maintains a blog condemning American imperialism, and Vinny is three-quarters into a Ph.D. in Black Studies. When Asuncion becomes their new roommate, the boys have a perfect opportunity to demonstrate how open-minded they truly are. "Mr. Eisenberg writes lively dialogue that strikes plenty of comic sparks." *—NY Times.* "An almost ridiculously enjoyable portrait of slacker trauma among would-be intellectuals." *—Newsday.* [2M, 2W] ISBN: 978-0-8222-2630-7

DRAMATISTS PLAY SERVICE, INC.
440 Park Avenue South, New York, NY 10016 212-683-8960 Fax 212-213-1539
postmaster@dramatists.com www.dramatists.com

NEW PLAYS

★ **THE PICTURE OF DORIAN GRAY by Roberto Aguirre-Sacasa, based on the novel by Oscar Wilde.** Preternaturally handsome Dorian Gray has his portrait painted by his college classmate Basil Hallwood. When their mutual friend Henry Wotton offers to include it in a show, Dorian makes a fateful wish—that his portrait should grow old instead of him—and strikes an unspeakable bargain with the devil. [5M, 2W] ISBN: 978-0-8222-2590-4

★ **THE LYONS by Nicky Silver.** As Ben Lyons lies dying, it becomes clear that he and his wife have been at war for many years, and his impending demise has brought no relief. When they're joined by their children all efforts at a sentimental goodbye to the dying patriarch are soon abandoned. "Hilariously frank, clear-sighted, compassionate and forgiving." –NY Times. "Mordant, dark and rich." –Associated Press. [3M, 3W] ISBN: 978-0-8222-2659-8

★ **STANDING ON CEREMONY by Mo Gaffney, Jordan Harrison, Moisés Kaufman, Neil LaBute, Wendy MacLeod, José Rivera, Paul Rudnick, and Doug Wright, conceived by Brian Shnipper.** Witty, warm and occasionally wacky, these plays are vows to the blessings of equality, the universal challenges of relationships and the often hilarious power of love. "CEREMONY puts a human face on a hot-button issue and delivers laughter and tears rather than propaganda." –BackStage. [3M, 3W] ISBN: 978-0-8222-2654-3

★ **ONE ARM by Moisés Kaufman, based on the short story and screenplay by Tennessee Williams.** Ollie joins the Navy and becomes the lightweight boxing champion of the Pacific Fleet. Soon after, he loses his arm in a car accident, and he turns to hustling to survive. "[A] fast, fierce, brutally beautiful stage adaptation." –NY Magazine. "A fascinatingly lurid, provocative and fatalistic piece of theater." –Variety. [7M, 1W] ISBN: 978-0-8222-2564-5

★ **AN ILIAD by Lisa Peterson and Denis O'Hare.** A modern-day retelling of Homer's classic. Poetry and humor, the ancient tale of the Trojan War and the modern world collide in this captivating theatrical experience. "Shocking, glorious, primal and deeply satisfying." –Time Out NY. "Explosive, altogether breathtaking." –Chicago Sun-Times. [1M] ISBN: 978-0-8222-2687-1

★ **THE COLUMNIST by David Auburn.** At the height of the Cold War, Joe Alsop is the nation's most influential journalist, beloved, feared and courted by the Washington world. But as the '60s dawn and America undergoes dizzying change, the intense political dramas Joe is embroiled in become deeply personal as well. "Intensely satisfying." –Bloomberg News. [5M, 2W] ISBN: 978-0-8222-2699-4

DRAMATISTS PLAY SERVICE, INC.
440 Park Avenue South, New York, NY 10016 212-683-8960 Fax 212-213-1539
postmaster@dramatists.com   www.dramatists.com

NEW PLAYS

★ **BENGAL TIGER AT THE BAGHDAD ZOO by Rajiv Joseph.** The lives of two American Marines and an Iraqi translator are forever changed by an encounter with a quick-witted tiger who haunts the streets of war-torn Baghdad. "[A] boldly imagined, harrowing and surprisingly funny drama." –*NY Times.* "Tragic yet darkly comic and highly imaginative." –*CurtainUp.* [5M, 2W] ISBN: 978-0-8222-2565-2

★ **THE PITMEN PAINTERS by Lee Hall, inspired by a book by William Feaver.** Based on the triumphant true story, a group of British miners discover a new way to express themselves and unexpectedly become art-world sensations. "Excitingly ambiguous, in-the-moment theater." –*NY Times.* "Heartfelt, moving and deeply politicized." –*Chicago Tribune.* [5M, 2W] ISBN: 978-0-8222-2507-2

★ **RELATIVELY SPEAKING by Ethan Coen, Elaine May and Woody Allen.** In TALKING CURE, Ethan Coen uncovers the sort of insanity that can only come from family. Elaine May explores the hilarity of passing in GEORGE IS DEAD. In HONEYMOON MOTEL, Woody Allen invites you to the sort of wedding day you won't forget. "Firecracker funny." –*NY Times.* "A rollicking good time." –*New Yorker.* [8M, 7W] ISBN: 978-0-8222-2394-8

★ **SONS OF THE PROPHET by Stephen Karam.** If to live is to suffer, then Joseph Douaihy is more alive than most. With unexplained chronic pain and the fate of his reeling family on his shoulders, Joseph's health, sanity, and insurance premium are on the line. "Explosively funny." –*NY Times.* "At once deep, deft and beautifully made." –*New Yorker.* [5M, 3W] ISBN: 978-0-8222-2597-3

★ **THE MOUNTAINTOP by Katori Hall.** A gripping reimagination of events the night before the assassination of the civil rights leader Dr. Martin Luther King, Jr. "An ominous electricity crackles through the opening moments." –*NY Times.* "[A] thrilling, wild, provocative flight of magical realism." –*Associated Press.* "Crackles with theatricality and a humanity more moving than sainthood." –*NY Newsday.* [1M, 1W] ISBN: 978-0-8222-2603-1

★ **ALL NEW PEOPLE by Zach Braff.** Charlie is 35, heartbroken, and just wants some time away from the rest of the world. Long Beach Island seems to be the perfect escape until his solitude is interrupted by a motley parade of misfits who show up and change his plans. "Consistently and sometimes sensationally funny." –*NY Times.* "A morbidly funny play about the trendy new existential condition of being young, adorable, and miserable." –*Variety.* [2M, 2W] ISBN: 978-0-8222-2562-1

DRAMATISTS PLAY SERVICE, INC.
440 Park Avenue South, New York, NY 10016 212-683-8960 Fax 212-213-1539
postmaster@dramatists.com   www.dramatists.com

NEW PLAYS

★ **CLYBOURNE PARK by Bruce Norris.** WINNER OF THE 2011 PULITZER PRIZE AND 2012 TONY AWARD. Act One takes place in 1959 as community leaders try to stop the sale of a home to a black family. Act Two is set in the same house in the present day as the now predominantly African-American neighborhood battles to hold its ground. "Vital, sharp-witted and ferociously smart." –*NY Times.* "A theatrical treasure...Indisputably, uproariously funny." –*Entertainment Weekly.* [4M, 3W] ISBN: 978-0-8222-2697-0

★ **WATER BY THE SPOONFUL by Quiara Alegría Hudes.** WINNER OF THE 2012 PULITZER PRIZE. A Puerto Rican veteran is surrounded by the North Philadelphia demons he tried to escape in the service. "This is a very funny, warm, and yes uplifting play." –*Hartford Courant.* "The play is a combination poem, prayer and app on how to cope in an age of uncertainty, speed and chaos." –*Variety.* [4M, 3W] ISBN: 978-0-8222-2716-8

★ **RED by John Logan.** WINNER OF THE 2010 TONY AWARD. Mark Rothko has just landed the biggest commission in the history of modern art. But when his young assistant, Ken, gains the confidence to challenge him, Rothko faces the agonizing possibility that his crowning achievement could also become his undoing. "Intense and exciting." –*NY Times.* "Smart, eloquent entertainment." –*New Yorker.* [2M] ISBN: 978-0-8222-2483-9

★ **VENUS IN FUR by David Ives.** Thomas, a beleaguered playwright/director, is desperate to find an actress to play Vanda, the female lead in his adaptation of the classic sadomasochistic tale *Venus in Fur.* "Ninety minutes of good, kinky fun." –*NY Times.* "A fast-paced journey into one man's entrapment by a clever, vengeful female." –*Associated Press.* [1M, 1W] ISBN: 978-0-8222-2603-1

★ **OTHER DESERT CITIES by Jon Robin Baitz.** Brooke returns home to Palm Springs after a six-year absence and announces that she is about to publish a memoir dredging up a pivotal and tragic event in the family's history—a wound they don't want reopened. "Leaves you feeling both moved and gratifyingly sated." –*NY Times.* "A genuine pleasure." –*NY Post.* [2M, 3W] ISBN: 978-0-8222-2605-5

★ **TRIBES by Nina Raine.** Billy was born deaf into a hearing family and adapts brilliantly to his family's unconventional ways, but it's not until he meets Sylvia, a young woman on the brink of deafness, that he finally understands what it means to be understood. "A smart, lively play." –*NY Times.* "[A] bright and boldly provocative drama." –*Associated Press.* [3M, 2W] ISBN: 978-0-8222-2751-9

DRAMATISTS PLAY SERVICE, INC.
440 Park Avenue South, New York, NY 10016 212-683-8960 Fax 212-213-1539
postmaster@dramatists.com   www.dramatists.com